BRITISH BIRDS
FROM NATURE

B. Ridgley 1978

BRITISH BIRDS FROM NATURE

Frances Mary Isabella Smith

Introduced by Ralph Whitlock

Hamlyn
London · New York · Sydney · Toronto

Text and illustrations Frances Mary Isabella Smith
©Robert Dorrien Smith 1985
Text and design ©Thames Head Limited 1985

First published 1985 by
The Hamlyn Publishing Group Limited
London · New York · Sydney · Toronto
Astronaut House, Feltham, Middlesex, England.

Published simultaneously in the USA
by Salem House.

ISBN 0 600 30620 8

Typeset by
SP Typesetting, Birmingham

Reproduction by
Redsend Limited, Birmingham

Printed in Great Britain by
Purnell & Sons Limited, Paulton

British Birds from Nature
was conceived, edited,
and designed by
Thames Head Limited,
Avening, Tetbury,
Gloucestershire,
Great Britain

Designer
Nick Allen

Editor
Alison Goldingham

CONTENTS

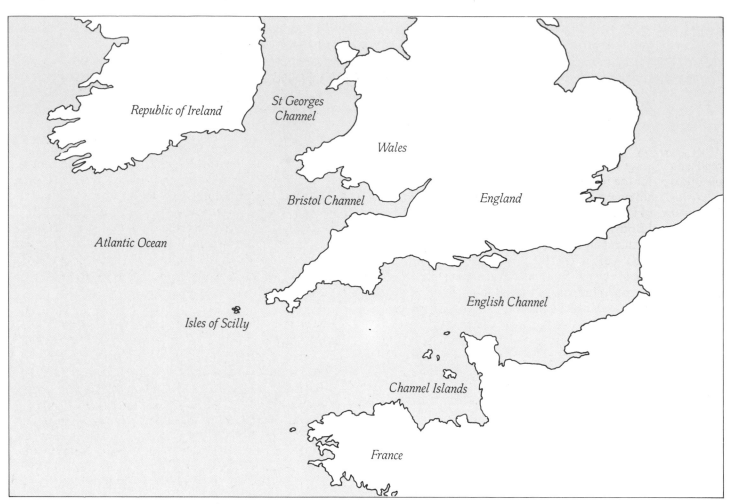

Republic of Ireland

St Georges
Channel

Wales

Bristol Channel

England

Atlantic Ocean

Isles of Scilly

English Channel

Channel Islands

France

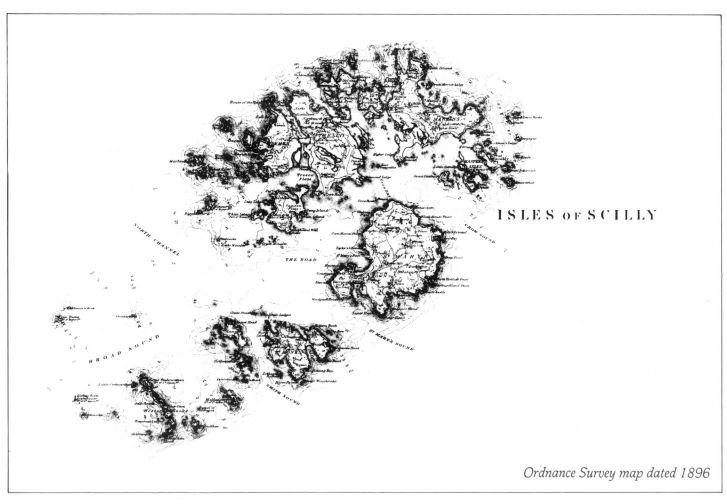

ISLES of SCILLY

Ordnance Survey map dated 1896

INTRODUCTION

Frances Mary Isabella Smith, to be known to our readers as Fanny, cannot be claimed as a pioneer of British ornithology, for the reason that her work has not been published until now and has been seen only by members of her family. However, she has a firm place in the second generation of British naturalists. Reverend Gilbert White, the father of British natural history, had been in his grave for only nineteen years when she was born in 1812, and while she was a schoolgirl Thomas Bewick was still engaged on his magnificent woodcuts. Many of his pictures had been published in his four-volume *History of British Birds (1797-1804),* setting a standard for meticulous accuracy combined with realistic vivacity which served as a pattern for subsequent nature artists, of whom Fanny was one. John Audubon, the great American artist, was another of Fanny's contemporaries. His monumental work, *The Birds of America,* which gives coloured portrayals of 1,065 birds, was completed in the year 1838, the year in which Fanny herself began her bird paintings. She may well have been familiar with his books, for she paid at least one visit to Canada.

The self-appointed task of the great Swedish naturalist, Linnaeus (1707-78), had also become sufficiently well known for Fanny to be acquainted with it. Though building on the foundations laid by the English naturalist, John Ray, of a century earlier, it was Linnaeus who devised the simple system of nomenclature which bears his name and which still prevails to this day. All living things are classified under order, family and so on, down to genus and species. The system is binomial, the first name indicating the genus, the second the species. Thus the Wagtails belong to the genus *Motacilla,* and the Yellow Wagtail is *Motacilla flava (flava* being Latin for yellow). A simple but efficient process. As a contemporary of Linnaeus expressed it: 'We have made so much progress that by his tables we can refer any fish, plant or mineral to its genus and subsequently to its species, even though none of us have seen it before.'

Fanny is entirely familiar with the system and uses it in all her paintings and notes, botanical as well as ornithological. A few decades before her time (in 1778) the Linnaean Society of London was founded, based on Linnaeus' enormous collection of insects, pressed plants, shells, minerals, numerous other specimens and quantities of manuscripts. They had been acquired, on the death of Linnaeus, in fierce competition with would-be purchasers in other countries, by a rich Englishman, James Edward Smith, who chartered a ship especially to bring the lot to England. Although there is no evidence of this, it is more than likely that Fanny knew of such a distinguished naturalist, especially as he had been the first President of the Linnaean Society and shared her father's name.

It was an age when men were reaching out to explore the natural secrets of the world. Linnaeus himself had sent out students to collect specimens and reports of the fauna and flora of such distant countries as India, Japan, Africa, South America, New Zealand and the Pacific Islands. It was largely due to his intervention that Sir Joseph Banks was allowed (at his own expense!) to accompany Captain James Cook on his voyage around the world. When Fanny was a girl Sir Joseph was still alive and President of the Royal Society.

The upsurge of interest in the natural world predictably inspired interpretation in art. Throughout the latter part of the eighteenth century the number of gifted botanical painters steadily increased. Two of the most talented, the Austrian brothers, Ferdinand and Francis Bauer, came to London in 1790, and, at Banks's suggestion and expense, Francis was appointed official draughtsman at Kew, a post he occupied for fifty years. Considered by some authorities to be the greatest botanical artist of all time, Francis Bauer, besides spending his time in the congenial occupation of recording in colour the plants brought to him from every part of the world, also gave lessons in botanical painting to Queen Charlotte (wife of King George III) and to several of her daughters.

The Queen had for a long time displayed a love for flowers. In the early days of her marriage she had planted a flower garden, well stocked with carnations, in the grounds of The Queen's House (now Buckingham Palace). Later she established her own botanic gardens near a new residence, the Dutch House at Richmond, which were eventually, in the reign of Queen Victoria, incorporated in the Royal Botanic Gardens. When her husband decided to take up residence in Windsor Castle, the dutiful Queen created at Frogmore 'My little Paradise', as she called it. Here she erected greenhouses, grew exotic flowers and also painted them. The botanist Dr R.J. Thornton, writing as a contemporary in 1812, says:

'There is not a plant in the Gardens of Kew . . . but has been either drawn by her gracious Majesty, or some of the Princesses, with a grace and skill which reflect on these personages the highest honour . . .' In short, the Queen and the Princesses set a fashion which was enthusiastically followed by a generation of society girls, among them Fanny. She, however, had more talent than most. She was also one of a far less numerous school who gave attention to birds and landscapes as well as flowers.

Material for the life story of this gifted woman is meagre. This is largely because after her death the Le Marchant family home and its contents, including her letters, family documents, photographs, notes and some of her paintings, were destroyed by fire. We know that she was born at Ashlyns Hall, near Berkhamsted, Hertfordshire, in 1812, three years before the Battle of Waterloo. She married Thomas Le Marchant (later Lieutenant Colonel Le Marchant), fifth son of Major General John Gaspard Le Marchant, in 1846. She was alive in 1903, as the only extant photograph of her was taken at a family gathering at Tresco in that year. Some of her descendants are still living in Lincolnshire.

Much of her life, however, was closely linked with that of her illustrious brother, Augustus Smith, a man of remarkable gifts who came to be known by some as The Governor, and by many more as The Emperor, of the Isles of Scilly. We can trace pieces of Fanny's history in incidental references to her in the correspondence by and about him. That is not to say that she was a nonentity, completely overshadowed by a famous brother. On the contrary, she seems to have possessed a measure of similar dynamism and imagination, and it is by no means certain that they got on well together all the time.

The Smiths were one of those families, plentiful in English history but rare in that of many other countries, which had risen from the ranks of humble artisans to become landed gentry. Some such families have subsequently taken pains to disguise their lowly origins by adopting new surnames, but Augustus Smith, on the contrary, was proud of his roots. He paid full tribute to them in a family history he caused to be compiled, entitled *A True and Faithful History of the Family of Smith, originally cradled at Wiverton and Cropwell Butler in the parish of Titheby and more recently established at Nottingham*. Taking a swipe at pretentions and snobbery, he declares,

'Had the vegetable creation any reasoning powers, one can imagine the feelings of superiority to which the Golden Pippin or Truro Gilliflower could be scarcely insensible when coming into contact with the crab of the hedges or even the uneatable cider-apple of the orchard; or how that Pharisee of strawberries, Myatt's Superb, might exult while he utters thanks that he is not as other strawberries are or even as the wild Publican of the woods . . .'

With that preamble Augustus takes a wholehearted delight in the enterprise and exploits of his sturdy ancestors, beginning with John Smith, who was a yeoman at the time of the commonwealth and whose grandfather was a smith by trade. By the early eighteenth century the family was well established as merchants in the city of Nottingham. One of them, Thomas, became High Sheriff of Nottingham and also founded the first provincial bank in England. In generation after generation the gifted and energetic Smiths multiplied their fortunes, until James, Augustus's father, inherited enough to invest in Ashlyns Hall and never to do a stroke of work for the rest of his life.

To James, however, Ashlyns Hall represented at first a refuge from the world. He was both married and widowed in the year 1800, his wife dying at the birth of their son ten months after the wedding. He and the little boy, another James, moved to Ashlyns in 1801. There he found himself surrounded by sympathetic neighbours who did their best to prevent him from becoming a recluse. Ashlyns, now a college and conference centre, is situated about a mile south of the little town of Berkhamsted and was one of a small galaxy of similar estates. Among them were Haresfoot, where the Dorrien family lived, Berkhamsted Hall, the home of the Pechells, and Gaddesden Place

Ashlyns Hall, Hertfordshire, taken at the beginning of this century

where the Halseys resided. All of these families made sure that James never missed out on an invitation to a social event. Considerably higher in the social scale, the eccentric and powerful Duke of Bridgewater lived in almost regal splendour at Ashridge, a magnificent mansion crowning the long, curving ridge on the opposite side of the valley.

The odds against a widower, aged thirty-one, possessed of a fine country house and a considerable fortune, maintaining his celibate state for long must have been extremely heavy, and Christmas 1803 saw James satisfactorily married to Mary Isabella Pechell, the twenty-year-old daughter of the Pechells of Berkhamsted Hall. Augustus, who tends to dominate this story, was born in the following September.

Ashlyns now became a true family home, filled with life and chatter. A second son, Frederick, was born in 1806; then, after a gap of six years, three younger children. They were Frances Mary Isabella (Fanny) in 1812, Robert Algernon in 1814, and finally, after another six-year gap, Paulina Wilhelmina in 1820. The family happiness was mixed with tragedy, for in 1811 James, the eldest boy, fell off his pony in the grounds of Ashlyns and was killed.

Fanny therefore never knew her eldest brother, but one can well imagine that she must have adored Augustus, the big brother eight years older than herself. He must have dominated life for her, at least in the holidays. He, and presumably Frederick as well, were educated at Harrow and Oxford, but it seems that the girls had a resident governess, a Miss Christian. She was still with them in 1843, when the survivors of the family left Ashlyns and moved to the Isles of Scilly.

By 1835, when Fanny was twenty-three, she was keeping house for her father at Ashlyns. It is recorded that she was a dashing, fearless horsewoman and a talented artist. Unfortunately, no portrait of her as a young woman survives, but there is one of her younger sister, Paulina, painted by a local artist, William Claridge, and Fanny is said to have closely resembled her. The Pechells were a dark-eyed Huguenot family and Paulina had large brown eyes, like her mother, and a mass of jet black curls. Paulina was apparently an intelligent, intellectual girl and a great favourite with her brother Augustus, whereas the energetic and forceful Fanny may have been too much like him for his comfort.

The only photograph we have of Fanny, reproduced on the page below, shows her at a family reunion to celebrate the return of General Dorrien Smith from the Boer War in the year 1903.

It was remembered long afterwards that in order to attend this gathering Fanny, then aged ninety-one, drove forty miles in an open, high-wheeled dog cart, with only one attendant. She also insisted on driving home again that same day.

A formidable lady indeed!

In the summer of 1835 Augustus sent for fifteen-year-old Paulina to visit him in the Isles of Scilly - the first member of the family to be invited to his new home. Preparations for the excursion lasted for weeks, and the long journey by stage-coach from London to Penzance must have been a tiring one. Paulina was entranced by what she saw on Tresco, where the new Tresco Abbey was being built.

Fanny (Mrs Thomas le Marchant), seated third from the left, pictured in 1903

Tragically, she caught a chill while watching the launching of a ship one evening and died only a few weeks later. Her body was taken back for burial in the family vault at Berkhamsted.

Meanwhile Frederick had entered the Army, which sent him to India where he died at the age of twenty in 1826. By the time old James Smith died at the age of seventy-five, in 1843, only Fanny, Robert (who was now Captain Robert Smith of the Third Royal Dragoons) and Miss Christian remained at Ashlyns.

Augustus sent for them to join him in the Scillies, closing down Ashlyns, which was thereafter let, though with the stipulation that the gardens and grounds lovingly fashioned by his mother were to remain unaltered. Whenever it became necessary for Augustus to busy himself with affairs at Berkhamsted, he did so from a base in London. Evidently some of the Ashlyns servants joined in the migration to the Isles of Scilly, for there is a later note to the effect that Holliday, the Scottish bailiff who had had charge of the farm at Ashlyns, was working for Augustus on Tresco but was 'only a tolerable agriculturist'.

But we are a little ahead of our story. What, it may be asked, was Augustus doing in the Isles of Scilly that seemed of such importance to him that he was willing to abandon his birthplace?

Augustus had inherited in good measure the energy and acumen of his Smith ancestors. The quiet life and trivial round of social events were not for him. From his mother's family he was endowed with a certain idealism, of the sort that had made them flee from France, under conditions of great hardship, when the persecution of Huguenots began. At Oxford he had taken little pleasure in the wild goings-on enjoyed by most undergraduates, and back at Ashlyns he found hunting, shooting, parties and balls boring. He wanted something to do, something to get his teeth into, but the normal incentive for an ambitious young man was lacking. His fortune was already made - and would be handed to him on a plate. Luckily he did not have to search far for inspiration.

Observant by nature, he took note of what was happening in and around Ashlyns. It did not take him long to discover that there were other ways of life than the social round followed by the country gentry. By contrast, most of the inhabitants of the countryside lived in broken-down hovels and were engaged in a desperate struggle with poverty. Farm workers were then living in the aftermath of the Speenhamland policy which, in 1795, had decreed that farm wages should be subsidized out of the parish rates. It was a good idea which worked out disastrously in practice. Farmers tended to give notice to all but their key workers immediately after harvest. The workers reported to the parish overseer, who sent them back to the same farmers. They were then re-engaged at the lowest possible wages, and the amount needed to keep them from starvation was made up from the parish rates. In consequence, the rates soared steadily, and both workers and ratepayers complained bitterly.

Fanny's elder brother Augustus Smith, a man of remarkable talent and vision

Augustus also discovered that there were two distinct types among the depressed poor. There were those who genuinely tried hard but were defeated by the system. And there were those who didn't bother to try. Prominent among the former were the nonconformists or dissenters, particularly the followers of John Wesley. Augustus felt that they owed their superiority to the fact that they had taken the trouble to improve their education.

Berkamsted had a fine old grammar school, founded and endowed by King Edward VI. For nearly a hundred years it had stood empty, though all that time each headmaster had regularly drawn his salary. A lawsuit was in progress to decide what should be done with the surplus cash that had accumulated.

Augustus found that most Berkhamsted children never attended school, so he proposed that the grammar school should be reopened for them. Or, alternatively, that parish schools with a sensible curriculum should be provided. The pupils should spend half their time at letters and figures, the other half at learning some useful trade or craft. At first the idea was greeted with enthusiasm, but that was before it was realised that Augustus was proposing that all children should get equal treatment. What! Educate the children of nonconformists side by side with Church children! That would never do!

Clergymen who had shown no interest in education for decades preached against the proposal, and at their instigation the gentry dipped their hands into their pockets. When Augustus went ahead with his parish schools, they reacted by opening a Church school. Undeterred, Augustus provided the necessary financial support for Berkhamsted parish school for nearly forty years. The controversy, however, became highly unpleasant. Augustus was vilified and ostracized. * Fanny must have been affected by this persecution, though whether she supported her brother or not we do not know.

* Such is the version of events given in the official biography of Augustus (*Augustus Smith of Scilly* by Elizabeth Inglis-Jones), but local histories of Berkhamsted and district tend to show at least some of the clergy and gentry in a somewhat better light. Augustus made enemies easily.

Although Augustus throve on opposition and was inflexible once he had made up has mind, he became exasperated with all the frustrations he encountered. Convinced that his ideas on universal education were right, he set his mind on finding a place where he could freely put his plans into practice. When he learned that the Lordship of the Isles of Scilly was about to become vacant, he applied and, after protracted negotiations, was granted a lease on the islands for three lives: ninety-nine years. He took possession in November 1834.

At the best of times the economy was hampered by the existence of an ancient practice whereby on his death the property of a peasant was divided equally among his heirs, resulting in the hopeless fragmentation of holdings into tiny strips of land. Moreover there were no written tenancy contracts, only verbal agreements which were fruitful territory for disputes.

The net result of all this was terrible hardship and privation, to the extent that both the government and

One of Fanny's flower paintings, 1879

The Tresco Abbey rock garden in its very early stages

Of all the dark corners of early nineteenth century England, the Isles of Scilly were among the most benighted. A cluster of tiny islands and rocks some thirty miles off Land's End, they were poverty-stricken, desolate and neglected. Apart from a clump in the sheltered Holy Vale on St Mary's, there was not a tree in the entire archipelago. In times of war the islands enjoyed brief periods of relative prosperity, serving as a base for guarding the western approaches to the English Channel, but in the intervals they lapsed into virtual dereliction. Smuggling became the chief industry, supplemented by the salvage of wrecks (some of which, it may be suspected, were lured to their doom). On dark nights the intrepid islanders thought little of venturing over to France and returning with cargoes of contraband brandy. Many of them were skilled pilots and, using their expertise legitimately, would guide ships safely past the islands and up the channel to English and continental ports.

The land surface of the islands was too small and rocky for the local harvest ever to be very reliable. There was a fluctuating trade in boat-building, and for a time a kelp-burning industry flourished to a modest degree, the kelp yielding ash for use in the manufacture of glass and soap. At the end of the Napoleonic Wars, however, this industry collapsed, and at the same time the government clamped down on smuggling and free-lance piloting.

private charities were constrained to send relief supplies of grain and money. Unhappily, it seems little of this charity got farther than the main island of St Mary's, which was least badly off, and the other islands continued to suffer.

Into this morass strode Augustus, with clearcut and confident ideas as to what he intended to do. First and foremost, he was determined that every child on the islands should receive a good education. Then a new system of land tenure had to be devised, and proper tenancy agrements drawn up. Smuggling was to be eradicated and replaced by well-paid work for everyone.

All these innovations were duly introduced and in time worked exceedingly well for the islanders, as the next generation of Scillonians gratefully admitted. At the time, however, every stage met determined opposition. True to his upbringing as an early nineteenth century country gentleman, Augustus didn't even pay lip-service to democracy. He was a thorough autocrat. Whatever he did was in his opinion best for the people of his new domain, and they had better agree! With industrious, hard-working folk who tried to improve their lot he had every sympathy and gave them every opportunity he could. But with ne'er-do-wells or those who tried to thwart him he could be completely ruthless. If they didn't like what he was doing, they could get out. Many of them did so.

11

The well-paid alternative to smuggling, which was part of his programme, was building. Within a very short time he had begun a new church on St Mary's, built a new pier and started the renovation and enlargement of Tresco Abbey, which overlooked the ruins of an old Benedictine monastery. Ship-building was revived, ships called with increasing frequency, and, as most people moved into paid employment, money began to circulate freely and new houses were soon being built everywhere. Above all, Augustus built schools. Forty years earlier than on the English mainland, attendance at school became compulsory on the Scillies. No one was stricter at enforcing the rule than Augustus himself. 'Old Caliban', truant children called him behind his back. To others he was 'The Governor' or 'The Emperor'.

Although the malcontents who were shipped back to the mainland would have disagreed, the results of this autocratic government were entirely beneficial. Among the subjects taught in the schools, appropriate to an island community, was navigation. As the first products of this novel programme went out into the world it was not long before Scillonian seamen earned a high reputation wherever they travelled. Very few of them remained deck-hands. They became pilots, master merchantmen, naval officers, captains of ships. Where else could ordinary seamen be found who were not only able to read and write but were also skilled in navigation? So obviously successful was the experiment that many young seamen, who had left the islands before schooling was available, came back and enrolled as pupils, studying with boys half their age. Augustus was delighted.

The rehabilitated Tresco Abbey was ready for occupation in 1838. For the rest of his life, which ended in 1872, Augustus was constantly improving his home estate on Tresco, his favourite island, and in particular establishing its superb sub-tropical gardens which are still such an enchanting feature.

As the years went by, his collection of exotic plants was continually being enhanced by specimens brought to him from every corner of the world by seafarers who had once been his pupils. Visitors to Tresco can still admire the tree-ferns, palms, escallonias, cacti, agaves, echeverias, the hedges of geraniums, fuchsias and euonymus and the many other tender plants so untypical of English gardens but so thoroughly at home in the Scillies. The Californian pines planted by his successor, Algernon Dorrien Smith, provide ideal shelter from the wild Atlantic gales.

This new interest in horticulture had an important commercial by-product. Before the Smith era the crofters of the Scillies had of necessity to rely quite heavily on their potato crop, which gave a higher yield of food per acre than did wheat and was also better suited to the climate. As life began to be better organized under Augustus and communications with the mainland easier and more frequent, they realised the advantage in being able to harvest very early crops, and so a trade in early potatoes and early vegetables developed. Eventually greater importance was placed on the trade in early spring flowers,

Augustus surrounded by the enchanting sub-tropical gardens he established on Tresco

started at the suggestion of Augustus in about 1867. The first bunches were sent to Covent Garden in a hat-box, but the early consignments were so popular that the trade proliferated until flowers were being despatched by the ton (650 tons were sent in 1895). Soon every smallholder in the islands was growing Soleil d'Or or Scilly White narcissi or some other early variety, and glasshouses were springing up in every sheltered corner.

The time has come to fit Fanny and her paintings into the picture. We have already noticed her as a girl at Ashlyns Hall, sharing the governess, Miss Christian, with her younger sister, Paulina, and later keeping house for her father until his death in 1843. It is likely that the majority of her bird portraits were executed during this period. Out of the thirty-six that have survived, fourteen are specifically stated to be birds 'procured' or 'obtained' at or near Ashlyns. Of the others many are of birds more likely to be found in Hertfordshire than in the Scillies. However, we cannot be sure, for her picture of a nightjar, essentially a woodland species, was painted from a bird shot in the Scillies, doubtless on migration. To her notes Fanny appends the information that it was depicted 'on a branch of a green aloe, the first that ever flowered there, 1845'.

Soon after the death of their father in 1843, as we know, Augustus let Ashlyns and transported the surviving members of his family to the Isles of Scilly. There Fanny evidently lived for at least some of the time till her marriage in 1846. She was present, therefore, during critical years when Augustus's venture was beginning to take shape. It might have been expected that, being a person of apparently much the same temperament as himself, she would have had a prominent share in events, but there is no mention of anything of the sort.

Fanny's artistic skill was not restricted to birds and flowers — here are two views of Tresco Abbey painted in 1870, showing the aspect from the Penzance Road and the entrance gateway

How did she meet and marry Lieutenant-Colonel Thomas Le Marchant? We do not know, but it seems that Augustus may not have approved of the match. When, nearly thirty years later, Augustus was on his death-bed in Plymouth and the Le Marchants came to see him, he would not allow Colonel Le Marchant to remain under the same roof but sent him packing to a hotel at Exeter.

We may assume that Fanny was reasonably happy, for she married into an artistic family. Her father-in-law, General John Gaspard Le Marchant, was an accomplished painter in water-colours, as was his other son, John Gaspard. His wife and his sister Elizabeth both did botanical studies, so Fanny would have had ample encouragement in continuing her work.

After her marriage Fanny accompanied her husband on tours of military duty. We have notes of her painting in Malta and Corfu, probably when he was fighting in the Crimean War. At some time, though we do not know when, she visited Canada.

In September 1867, she was back in Tresco, though whether with or without her husband we cannot be sure. A note of that date states:
Augustus's sister Fanny, Mrs Frances Isabella Le Marchant, now began to spend some of her time painting the Abbey and its gardens, and the flowers which grew in it, leaving an invaluable record of Augustus's creation.

These are said to have been 'the first dated paintings'.

From that time onwards, Fanny was there for several autumns - certainly in September 1868 and September 1870 (when she painted seven landscapes in a month).

13

Augustus died in 1872. Fanny was present for his last few days, at the Duke of Cornwall's Hotel at Plymouth. In his last letter, dated July 19th 1872, he wrote, 'I am particularly comfortable here with everything I can want and very nice. The Le Marchants offered to join me but I am better alone, talking being inconvenient.' Nevertheless, the Le Marchants did come, only to be greeted by The Emperor's wrath. They had disobeyed orders. He allowed Fanny to stay, though she could only enter his room when he sent for her, but he would not see the Colonel. To avoid friction Colonel Le Marchant retired to Exeter.

After Augustus's death, Fanny was more frequently in the Scillies. Says a contemporary record, 'Over the next ten years she created an invaluable record of what were the chief attractions of the garden.' In all she completed forty-four paintings, featuring more than 180 plants. In the early part of the period the paintings are dated September/October or March/April, but from 1875 onwards there are some done in summer as well, so she may well have become a permanent resident.

The bird paintings executed in the Isles of Scilly belong either to Fanny's early residence there, before her marriage, or to this latter period, post-1867. In spite of the fact that some of them have a date in the 1840s appended, we may assume that most of them belong to her later life. There are certain pointers in that direction. Three of the rarities, namely, Bee-eater, Roller and Rose-coloured Pastor, are stated to be birds shot in the Scillies and to be in the collection of Mr E.H. Rodd, of Penzance.

Edward Hearle Rodd; the historian for Cornwall, who rescued many rare birds from oblivion

We know more of Edward Hearle Rodd than we do of Fanny; he was quite a notable character. The younger son of a Cornish squire, he was a solicitor by profession, a classical scholar, an inspector of schools and an assistant poor-law commissioner. He was of the same age as Augustus and shared many of his ideas about education. One gathers that he and Augustus first met when the latter was transporting his family to the Scillies in 1843. The two men immediately took to each other, and Rodd was soon invited over to the Scillies to see what Augustus was up to. They became great friends, and Rodd was one of the last persons to visit Augustus on his death-bed.

During the middle years of the nineteenth century most English counties produced an ornithologist who compiled a history of the county's birds. The general pattern was that birds were shot (especially the rare varieties), had their skins stuffed and mounted, and the ornithologist provided each specimen with a detailed annotation, prepared a scientifically arranged list for the county, and finally published his findings in a book entitled *The Birds of ......* Edward Hearle Rodd was the historian for Cornwall. He made an impressive collection of the county's birds, including birds of the Scillies. His collection is still in existence, though in private hands. He had the firm of Trubner publish his *Birds of Cornwall* in 1880.

Probably because of his friendship with Augustus and the fact that he was so frequently in the islands, he also accumulated a lot of material for *The Birds of the Scillies*. He must have realised that the islands were an exceptional place for migrating birds, and today few ornithologists would contest the claim that they are the best in Europe. At any one time during the autumn there are now around 800 bird-watchers on the islands, an influx of visitors which is having a considerable influence on the economy.

In 1854 Rodd prepared (in manuscript form) a preliminary document entitled *The Ornithology of Scilly. A List of the various Birds that have been obtained on the Islands*. It is unsigned, but we know it is his work, for the handwriting corresponds to that in some of his surviving letters to Augustus Smith. The list comprises the impressive total of 168 species, a quite outstanding number considering that it was the harvest of occasional visits over less than ten years.

From the point of view of *Fanny's Birds* it has one significant inclusion and two omissions. The inclusion is the Rose-coloured Pastor, concerning which Edward Rodd wrote in 1854: 'A specimen was obtained a few years ago'. This is almost certainly the one which Fanny painted.

The omissions are the Bee-eater and the Roller. Neither bird appears in the list, which means that to that date they had not been recorded in the Scillies. Therefore Fanny's date (1845), and her statement, that her Bee-eater was shot in the Isles of Scilly and is in the collection of Mr Rodd of Penzance, must be wrong. The likely explanation is that Fanny did not write her notes at the time she painted her pictures , but at a later date and that her memory, after a lapse of perhaps many years, was faulty.

Fam. CORACIIDÆ.

ROLLER. *Coracias garrula*, Linn.

As a straggler this very handsome bird occasionally, though rarely, visits Cornwall. I have notes of its occurrence at the Land's End, St. Levan, St. Just, and near the Logan Rock, but the specimens obtained were generally in immature plumage. Dr. Bullmore has recorded a specimen of this bird killed at Falmouth in October 1842.

———

Fam. ALCEDINIDÆ.

KINGFISHER. *Alcedo ispida*, Linn.

On the sea coast, and especially at the mouths of rivers and estuaries, as well as in creeks, the Kingfisher may be often observed; its bright plumage rendering it at once a conspicuous and attractive object.

———

Fam. MEROPIDÆ.

BEE-EATER. *Merops apiaster*, Linn.

This brightly plumaged and remarkable bird can only be included as an accidental and rare visitor. In 1828, a flock appeared near Helston, and twelve

which were killed came into the possession of the late Mr. George Borlase of that place. Four others, according to Couch, were seen in the parish of Madron.

———

Fam. HIRUNDINIDÆ.

SWALLOW. *Hirundo rustica*, Linn.

A common summer visitant. The following entry in my note-book, under date 11th April 1872, may be worth transcribing :—

"A large arrival of Swallows was noticed yesterday afternoon at the Land's End, consisting of several troops of forty or fifty flying with considerable rapidity, and without, apparently, fatigue or exhaustion. Their direction was from the south-west, between the Scilly Isles and the Wolf Rock; time, 5 P.M. Many were afterwards flushed from furzy ground, exhibiting a somewhat feeble flight."

In November 1852, a circumstance was mentioned to me which may be regarded as interesting and worth recording, as coming from a naturalist whose general accuracy may be depended on implicitly. Mr. Vingoe, whose name has been frequently mentioned, introduced the subject by remarking that he had a strong suspicion that he had observed, towards the end of the previous summer, the Rufous Swallow. His attention was directed for some time to an individual, amongst several others, that appeared to

---

Rodd's entries on the Bee-eater and the Roller reproduced from his 'Birds of Cornwall and the Scilly Islands' published in 1880

This notion is borne out by her reference to having seen the Waxwing (Waxen Chatterer) in Canada, which must have been later than the 1844 date attached to the painting. Her notes on the Bee-eater bear the mark of personal observation, and she doubtless became acquainted with these birds in Malta and perhaps other Mediterranean countries after her marriage.

There remain three specimens identified as belonging neither to Ashlyns nor the Isles of Scilly. They are the Tree Sparrow, the Reed Bunting and the Sedge Warbler, all of which were shot either 'on the banks of the Severn' or 'in Worcestershire', which may well mean the same place. The link here is with Fanny's Aunt Augusta, the widow of Bishop Jenkinson, Bishop of St David's. She and her two daughters were among the family party which migrated to the Scillies when Ashlyns was closed in 1843. In October of that year they left Tresco, and it is recorded that 'a few days later everyone else went away, leaving the Abbey to be shut up for the winter.' Though the Smiths were back in the spring, it seems that Aunt Augusta settled in Worcestershire, for there is a record of Augustus visiting an aunt (thought to be this one) there in August 1858. Evidently Fanny also paid a visit to her aunt in Worcestershire and while there painted three bird pictures.

Such is the sum total of our information about the life and works of Frances Mary Isabella Smith (later Le Marchant)

one of the earliest painters of British birds. As a young woman she was swept up in the current vogue of flower-painting and proved to be a remarkably talented practitioner. Unlike most of her contemporaries, however, who stiltedly followed the fashion set by the late Queen Charlotte and the Princesses, she broke away to engage in her own passion for ornithology, an infant science of which she reveals a surprising knowledge.

Although it seems probable that much, perhaps most, of her ornithological work was done before her marriage in 1846, she evidently retained her interest in birds throughout her long life. It seems almost certain that some of the Isles of Scilly birds were painted when she was at Tresco between the years 1867 and 1883, recording in colour her brother's marvellous collection of exotic plants. By that time Rodd's impressive collection of birds would have been available to her, and the surprising thing is that she did not make more use of it. Of course, it could well be that she intended to do more but became so preoccupied with the flowers that she never got around to it.

Had her work been published at the time the paintings were executed, especially those of the early period, she would undoubtedly have earned a place as one of the pioneers of British ornithology. It is left to our generation to enjoy her inspired and delicate artistry and to pay tribute to its excellence.

LIST OF BIRD ENTRIES

in alphabetical order

Snow Bunting *Plectrophenax nivalis*

This bird's breeding range does extend to Britain, but only through a few pairs nesting on the highest Scottish mountains. It never perches on trees simply because it never sees any, except on its winter wanderings.

The bird Fanny portrays is in winter plumage; in summer the male appears in much bolder black and white. In winter small flocks, and sometimes quite large ones, are widespread along the east coasts of Scotland and England, but the specimen shot in the Isles of Scilly in 1839 would have been a rare find. An unknown writer of the 1850s records that in the Scillies, 'several specimens were obtained in the autumn of 1851 and a few in the autumn of 1854'. Its appearances so far to the south-west are very irregular. The reference to the nest being lined with deer's hair suggests that Fanny gleaned her information from Scotland, though whether through her own observation or second-hand we cannot tell.

Reed Bunting *Emberiza schoeniclus*

If we accept that 'grain' includes the seeds of various wild plants, Fanny's notes on the Reed Bunting are perfectly accurate.

These days the bird occurs more frequently in dry situations, such as chalk downs, sometimes even in the summer. This is possibly due to the destruction of many of its former marshy or riparian habitats.

Fanny's painting, depicting the bird perched on a Club Rush, illustrates that the former country name of this species, the 'Water Sparrow', was very apt.

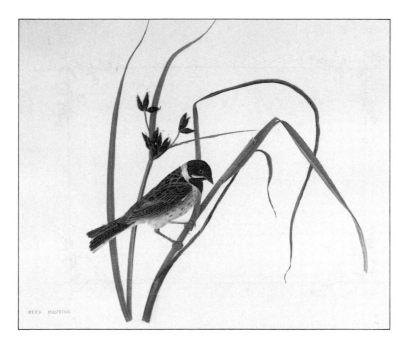

Lesser Redpole now known as
Redpoll or Lesser Redpoll *Acanthis flammea*

Fanny is either mis-informed about the status of the Redpoll in the British Isles or, which seems more likely, there has been a change since her day. Far from being confined to the northern counties of Scotland in the breeding season, the species occurs in most counties of Britain and Ireland, and its breeding population is estimated at around 600,000 pairs. Nesting starts rather earlier than Fanny implies, and there are sometimes two broods. I think she is wrong in stating that the birds often eat the buds of trees. They feed on seeds, except in spring when they feed their young on insects.

The Redpoll has several races or subspecies. The Lesser Redpoll (the British variety) is smaller and darker than some of its subspecies. However, contrary to what Fanny says, the female Lesser Redpoll does have some red on her head.

Common Linnet
Linnet *Acanthis cannabina*

Like the Goldfinch, the Linnet was a popular cage-bird in Victorian times and suffered accordingly. Fanny notes, however, that Linnets are abundant in the Isles of Scilly, as they are still, and in most other similar habitats. On cultivated land their status has declined a little, but they may still be seen in large flocks in winter.

The male Linnet does not entirely lose the crimson on his breast in winter, though it is much paler than in summer.

RED BREASTED LINNET

GOLDFINCH.

Goldfinch *Carduelis carduelis*

The capture of Goldfinches for cage-birds was a flourishing industry in Fanny's time. Very large numbers were caught by liming, nets and decoys, and bird-catchers constructed little traps around nests so that the young birds, although prevented from flying, could still be fed by their parents. Most cottages, and many larger residences, kept a captive Goldfinch, often in a cage far too small for it. The activities of bird-catchers brought the Goldfinch population to a dangerously low level, but since the species has been protected it has achieved a satisfactory status and is now widespread and not uncommon, although some illicit trapping is still alleged to take place. A writer in the mid-nineteenth century classifies the status of the Goldfinch in the Isles of Scilly as 'an autumn and winter visitor in small numbers.'

The 'willow down' mentioned by Fanny is the downy substance covering the catkins of willow and sallow. Fanny's Goldfinch is depicted perching on a Berberis twig.

Hawfinch *Coccothraustes coccothraustes*

Fanny categorizes this species as being not very common, and that is certainly true today. However, the bird is so shy and retiring that its status in any district is difficult to determine. Fanny mentions that her specimen was shot at Ashlyns, in Hertfordshire. In her other base, the Isles of Scilly, it would be only a very rare wanderer on migration, but one was seen in the Abbey Gardens on Tresco in October 1854 and two were reported on St Mary's at about the same time.

The Hawfinch has certainly been known to play havoc with green peas, but its lack of numbers means this is not a serious problem. While it is partial to hornbeam seeds, as Fanny states, it is equally fond of the stones and kernels of other hard seeds, particularly cherries, cracking even the hardest of these with its powerful bill.

HAWFINCH

Bullfinch *Pyrrhula pyrrhula*

Fanny's description of the Bullfinch and its habits is remarkably accurate, in view of the early date at which she is writing. She is wrong about there being only one brood; two are frequent, and occasionally there are three. The nesting season extends from the end of April to July, and the incubation period is twelve to fourteen days.

Although, as she observes, Bullfinches can quite easily be taught to whistle short tunes, in the wild they normally use only a low-pitched, piping whistle. They also have a song of sorts, consisting of whistles, warbles and wheezings, which they use only infrequently and which can be heard only at close range.

Modern writers tend towards the view that Bullfinches do pair for life, as Fanny suggests, though evidence is hard to come by.

Bramble Finch or Mountain Finch now known as Brambling *Fringilla montifringilla*

Since Fanny's day one pair of Bramblings is known to have nested in Scotland (in Sutherland in 1920) and there are unconfirmed reports of others in Scottish mountain districts. Apart from this, Fanny's observations hold good. Although the Brambling does occur in flocks, the flocks are usually of Chaffinches and Bramblings, with the Chaffinches predominant.

Fanny has chosen the posture of her Brambling carefully, the spread wings reveal the two chief identification features, namely, the white rump and the white bars on the wings, though she does not mention them in the text.

Chaffinch *Fringilla coelebs*

The Chaffinch is indeed one of our commonest birds, being more widespread than even the House Sparrow, which is normally confined to the vicinity of human habitations, whereas the Chaffinch is more ubiquitous. With an estimated population of some seven million pairs, its numbers are equalled only by the Blackbird.

Fanny's comments are accurate. Some writers have been impressed by the fact that seed-eating Chaffinches and other finches know instinctively that seeds are unsuitable food for their nestlings and so feed them with insects. However, very few seeds are available for food in spring and early summer, when the nestlings are about. Fanny rightly notes that at this season the adults too feed mostly on insects.

Tree Sparrow *Passer montanus*

Fanny illustrates the differences in plumage between the Tree Sparrow and the much more abundant House Sparrow but does not mention them in her notes. Besides being a rather smaller bird, the Tree Sparrow has a chestnut rather than a grey cap, a less extensive black bib and a black patch on the white cheek. The cheek is usually whiter and the patch more pronounced than in Fanny's picture. Also both sexes are alike, and the juveniles resemble their parents, in marked contrast to the females and young of the House Sparrow.

The Tree Sparrow is not as rare as Fanny implies, but its distribution is patchy and it is entirely absent from some areas. It has, however, been increasing and extending its range, particularly northwards and westwards. In winter it occurs in flocks, sometimes with other sparrows and finches.

Common Sparrow now known as
House Sparrow *Passer domesticus*

Fanny's choice of setting for this picture suggests that the painting was done in the Isles of Scilly, where stone walls and pennywort abound.

Her statement that white and buff-coloured varieties of this bird are not uncommon is interesting. In more than fifty years of bird-watching I have seen only one or two white sparrows and never a buff-coloured one. Were they more in evidence in Fanny's day, or was her observation at fault?

Nuthatch *Sitta europaea*

Here Fanny reveals a remarkable knowledge of the habits and behaviour of a not very abundant species. She knows about the Nuthatch's habit of reducing the size of its nesting hole by plastering mud around it. She knows, too, about how the Nuthatch wedges a nut into a crevice in tree bark before assailing the shell with hammer-like blows.

The number of eggs per clutch is more variable than she suggests, being sometimes as many as ten or twelve. The Nuthatch also has quite a variety of call-notes.

Fanny has chosen a not very typical setting for her bird, the flowers being of the rather unusual garden creeper, Thunbergia.

Bearded Titmouse now known as
Bearded Tit *Panurus biarmicus*

The Bearded Tit has become much scarcer since Fanny's day, largely owing to the draining of the Fens, which were its habitat, and also, to some extent, to the activities of collectors. Whittlesey Mere, formerly covering some 1500 acres, was drained in 1850. Its former site, like the Fens of Lincolnshire, is now flat and highly cultivated arable land. The breeding population of the Bearded Tit in Britain is now estimated at less than 500 pairs, most of which are found in the Norfolk Broads region and in neighbouring parts of Norfolk and Suffolk. After the breeding season the Bearded Tit tends to wander to suitable districts, characterized by dense reed-beds, in some of which small numbers of breeding pairs have established themselves in recent years.

Fanny is right in her description of nests and eggs, though modern textbooks put the number of eggs as between five and seven. Fanny says the nest is generally placed near the ground, but in fact, it is often built over water.

In depicting the bird perched on a Rosa Mundi Fanny has taken full artistic licence. It would never happen in nature, and the bird is in an unnatural posture. It is more likely to be found clinging upright to a reed stem.

Long Tailed Titmouse now known as
Long-tailed Tit *Aegithalos caudatus*

The Long-tailed Tit is now less common than Fanny implies it was in her day. It is one of those rather delicate species which experiences heavy mortality during a severe winter, after which it takes several years to recover its numbers.

Fanny's delightful description of the nest is accurate, but we now know that both sexes participate in nest building. Twelve eggs are about the maximum number, but sometimes there are as few as seven or eight. Insects and their larvae are the chief diet of Long-tailed Tits, (though in this context the term 'insects' should also include spiders) and they occasionally pick up seeds also.

Fanny's statement that, 'this bird has several notes, on the sound of which they assemble', might be misconstrued. As she says, these tits are almost incessantly in motion, and the little notes they utter as they flit through trees and bushes help them to keep in touch.

Greater Titmouse now known as
Great Tit *Parus major*

The Great Tit is not nearly such a confirmed cannibal as Fanny implies. It has been known to kill young birds in the nest, attacking them and pecking out their brains as Fanny describes, but this behaviour is by no means common.

Fanny omits to mention the pleasure in watching the antics of either this species or the Blue Tit, and nothing is said about bird tables or nest-boxes. Such developments lay in the future.

Fanny's picture does not show the black vertical band down the centre of the breast, which is one of the chief identification features. The bird is perched on an ornamental Crab Apple tree.

Common Wren
Wren *Troglodytes troglodytes*

Fanny is mistaken here in including worms in the food of the familiar Wren. Insects are its diet. Also there are often fewer eggs in the nest than she states - perhaps only five or six.

She is right about there being two broods and also that nest-building begins early. What she probably did not know is that the male often builds several nests, known as 'cock nests', from which the female selects one and lines it with feathers.

Her Wren and Blue Tit are depicted on the branch of an orange bush, with which she was probably familiar in the sub-tropical gardens of Tresco. Modern naturalists do not confirm her statement that the plumage of the female is of a redder tinge than that of the male.

Lesser Titmouse now known as
Blue Tit *Parus caeruleus*

Fanny's observations include nothing of the delight in the acrobatic antics of Blue Tits just outside the house windows. There are evidently no bird-tables or strings of peanuts in Fanny's gardens.

Where large numbers of eggs have been found in one nest, such as the eighteen that Fanny quotes, it is probable that two females have been using the same nest.

Referring to her statement that 'in winter they take to farmyards and outhouses', it may be worth remembering that in her day many farm outbuildings, as well as the ricks in the farmyards, were thatched, and the eaves of the thatch provided ideal roosting places for tits and other birds on winter nights.

Robin *Erithacus rubecula*

The reference to the 'endearing' qualities of the Robin is one of the few passages in which Fanny reveals a real feeling for birds, and she has captured admirably the perky stance of the Robin.

Her surmise that Robins pair for life is probably incorrect. Robins start to pair off soon after midwinter, the female selecting a mate from the available males. As for her statement that the behaviour of singing Robins is a reliable aid to forecasting the weather, it is this sort of information that does not find its way into modern books on birds. Nevertheless, it may be true.

Fanny's mention of a Robin building a nest behind books in a library sounds as though it comes from personal experience.

Redstart *Phoenicurus phoenicurus*

When Fanny mentions gardens as one of the Redstart's habitats she has in mind country house gardens, not the modern suburban type. It is also found in old parkland and in open country in hilly districts, where it nests in holes in stone walls. Since Fanny's day the Redstart has become less common in southern and eastern England.

A naturalist in the Isles of Scilly in the 1850s states that 'a few have been seen in the autumnal migration. All that have been noticed here have been females.' Probably we should add 'or juveniles', for young Redstarts are very like their mothers.

Stonechat *Saxicola torquata*

The Stonechat has declined considerably in numbers since Fanny's journal, for reasons not properly understood. It is now found chiefly in coastal and hill districts and shows a preference for uncultivated land.

Although Fanny is factual, as usual, in her descriptions of nest, eggs and nestlings, she is somewhat vague about dates, which are more elastic than she suggests. Egg-laying can begin as early as late March, and the incubation period is fourteen to fifteen days. The birds usually have a second brood, sometimes a third, and so they are often busy with their nests well into June.

Their food is mainly insects, with worms very much a subsidiary food.

Golden Crested Wren now known as
Goldcrest *Regulus regulus*

The Goldcrest appears to be much more plentiful now than at the time Fanny was writing. A survey undertaken by the British Trust for Ornithology from 1968-72 gave an estimated population of 1½ million for the British Isles (including Ireland). Because it is resident all the year round this species suffers severely in hard winters.

As usual, Fanny gives an accurate description of the nest. Modern authorities, however, give the bird an entirely insectivorous diet (spiders also included!).

The Pelargonium on which the birds are perching helps to make an attractive picture but it is an unlikely setting.

Yellow Wren now known as
Willow Warbler or Willow Wren
Phylloscopus trochilus

The Willow Warbler is much more common than Fanny apparently realized. A summer visitor, as she rightly says, it is found in almost every part of the British Isles, and it now has a breeding population estimated at over three million pairs. It is unlikely that Fanny differentiated between this species and the near-related Chiffchaff and Wood Warbler.

As to be expected, Fanny's descriptions of the nest and nesting habits are correct. To her notes on the song it could be added that the notes almost invariably follow a cascading pattern.

To picture a Willow Warbler on a berry-bearing branch of holly, as Fanny has done, is a little incongruous, but it can sometimes happen that holly berries are showing red before the last Willow Warblers depart for Africa.

Whitethroat *Sylvia communis*

The Whitethroat can now hardly be described as plentiful, even in southern England. Its decline in recent years is probably due to conditions in its winter quarters of West Africa, which have been increasingly affected by drought. Fanny's statement that the species winters in the southern countries of Europe is not quite correct, though perhaps a few birds occasionally do so.

As usual, Fanny's description of nest and eggs is entirely accurate. In her day, and for long afterwards, the word 'procured' was a euphemism for 'shot'!

Blackcap *Sylvia atricapilla*

There has been no change to Fanny's portrayal of this species, except that individuals more frequently overwinter in England. Few winters pass without some sightings of birds at bird-tables in south-western counties and sometimes farther north. As Fanny says, the Blackcap's song is strong and varied, being only inferior to that of the Nightingale, and in some places it was known in her day as the Northern Nightingale.

Sedge Warbler *Acrocephalus schoenobaenus*

In setting up these specimens for painting, Fanny has made them rather too elongated. The Sedge Warbler is a slightly more stumpy bird, with a shorter body and tail.

Although Fanny gives priority to worms as a food of this species, they are, in fact, of only minor importance; the bird is almost entirely insectivorous. Otherwise, Fanny's notes are as reliable as ever, and it is interesting that, only a hundred or so years after Gilbert White was speculating about swallows hibernating in the mud at the bottom of ponds, Fanny is aware that the Sedge Warbler is a migrant and has correctly placed the approximate dates of arrival and departure.

The Sedge Warbler is less exclusive to rivers, lakes and marshes than Fanny indicates. It is sometimes found in dry, bushy country well away from water - but perhaps this is a more recent development.

Waxen Chatterer now known as (Bohemian) Waxwing *Bombycilla garrulus*

This Isles of Scilly specimen has been delightfully painted to show the red wax-like tips to the secondary wing-feathers. Fanny mentions that she saw Waxwings on her visit to Canada, the species being found all round the northern rim of the northern temperate zone.

The Waxwing is one of those species which from time to time experience a 'population explosion', following a series of favourable breeding seasons. This results in spectacular irruptions of the species into Britain. Flocks of considerable size may appear in autumn, roaming the countryside and descending on suburban gardens to feed on ornamental berries. These invasion years may be followed by others in which very few Waxwings occur.

The picture is another example of artistic licence, the Waxwing would not be found in Britain when the Mallow was in bloom.

Rose Pastor now known as
Rose-coloured Pastor or Rose-coloured Starling
Sturnus roseus

Fanny is well aware that she has encountered a real rarity in this bird. Since her day it has been recorded more frequently in the British Isles and is now classified as an irregular visitor. Its home is in southern Russia, Turkey and the Caucasus, so specimens that occur in Britain are well off track. When the bird does appear it is usually in company with the related Starling, in flocks at the end of summer. Juveniles lack the brilliant colours of the adult male and look very like juvenile Starlings, so they may occur more frequently than is recorded.

Grey Wagtail *Motacilla cinerea*

Although her painting of the Grey Wagtail is accurate, it seems likely that Fanny failed to differentiate between this species and the Yellow Wagtail. Her comment that the bird lives in marshes and water-meadows and that the nest 'is placed on the ground, seldom distant from a stream and concealed by the inequalities of the ground', applies perfectly to the Yellow Wagtail but only to a limited extent to the Grey Wagtail. The Grey Wagtail likes swiftly flowing water and so is largely confined to the western half of Britain. Its nest is usually found in a hole in the bank of a mountain stream or in a wall or under a bridge. The details of the nest construction and of the number and colour of the eggs are accurate.

The reference to 'lines' applies to an obsolete measurement, a 'line' being one-twelfth of an inch.

Yellow Wagtail *Motacilla flava*

Once again Fanny is evidently well aware that she is recording a summer migrant. The alternative name of Ray's Wagtail is a tribute to the naturalist John Ray, who died in 1705 and who defined the species.

Unfortunately the Yellow Wagtail has declined quite drastically in numbers and distribution and is now considered rare in most districts, except in Yorkshire and its neighbouring counties. Amateur bird-watchers quite often report Yellow Wagtails in winter, but these are almost certainly the more plentiful Grey Wagtails, which also have yellow in their plumage.

Meadow Pepit now known as
Meadow Pipit *Anthus pratensis*

Fanny's statement that, 'This is the smallest and most common of this species', is not very helpful. In the more precise context of modern ornithology she means 'genus' - the genus *Anthus* - not the species. In fact there are three species of Pipit nesting in the British Isles: the Meadow Pipit, the Tree Pipit and the Rock Pipit, and there is very little difference in their size, though if one gets down to the accurate measurements of dead specimens the Meadow Pipit is certainly a little smaller than the other two.

The food of the Meadow Pipit consists of insects to a far greater extent than worms and slugs, though these are taken.

The 'Convolvolus' depicted by Fanny is the Sea Bindweed, which now bears the botanical name of *Calystegia soldanella*.

Greater Spotted Woodpecker now known as
Great Spotted Woodpecker *Dendrocopos major*

Fanny is evidently quite familiar with this bird and its habits. Since her time, however, the 'drumming' performance of woodpeckers has been more intensively studied. What Fanny describes as 'a quick tremulous motion of the head' is, in fact, the delivery of a rapid succession of hammer-like blows with the bill. The normal frequency is eight to ten blows per second. 'A sound as if the tree was splitting', is a good description.

Fanny was wrong about the purpose of the drumming, however. It is a performance associated with courtship and occurs only during the courting period, normally from February to early May.

If anything, the Great Spotted Woodpecker is even more widespread and plentiful than in Fanny's day, and, in general, it seems to be far less shy.

Roller *Coracias garrulus*

Here we have another brightly coloured and spectacular rarity. The species nests further north in central Europe than does the Bee-eater, even appearing in Scandinavia and Finland, but it is rarely found in north-western Europe and there are no records of breeding in Britain.

It is not completely true to say that the male is only distinguished from the female by its long outside tail feathers. Those feathers, which are black-tipped, are only slightly longer than the rest of the tail. The parts of the plumage that are turquoise in the male are a light chestnut-brown, tinged with blue in the female. The outer tail feathers lack the black tips. It is difficult to be sure, but Fanny's bird seems to be a female.

The Roller gets its name from the male's tendency when displaying, to engage in somersaults and tumbling from a considerable height.

Bee Eater now known as
Bee-eater *Merops apiaster*

Although the Bee-eater is a bird of the Mediterranean, a few individuals wander northwards, usually in spring, and find their way to the British Isles. Most southern and south-eastern counties of England have a few records of the species. A pair attempted to nest near Edinburgh in 1920, and a pair did so successfully in Sussex in 1955.

Fanny's description of the bird's behaviour and habits bears the mark of an eyewitness, but perhaps she copied them from the notes of another observer.

Kingfisher *Alcedo atthis*

As usual, most of Fanny's statements are quite accurate. Kingfishers do occasionally make use of ready-made holes by the water-side, but we now know that they often dig their own hole with both sexes participating. The hole is normally one-and-a-half to three feet deep, and, as Fanny says, the nest consists simply of a mass of foul-smelling fish-bones.

Here again we meet the obsolete measurement, the 'line' (one-twelfth of an inch). Fanny rightly notes that the eggs are almost spherical, from which one can infer that she has been doing some egg collecting!

Nightjar *Caprimulgus europaeus*

Yarret is a mistake for Yarrell, a pioneer British ornithologist who died in 1856. Perhaps one could quibble about his statement that it is the *only* nocturnal summer visitor, if the Nightingale is reckoned as a night bird.

In Fanny's last sentence the phrase 'now they are common in the islands' refers to the Aloes, not to the Nightjars, which have probably never been more than occasional visitors on migration. In mainland Britain, however, Nightjars are reasonably widespread in suitable country, and Fanny's comments are correct. Her picture accurately depicts the bird perching *along* the branch rather than *across* it, one of the few birds to do so.

Ringed Plover *Charadrius hiaticula*

Here Fanny at last turns her attention to shore birds and sea birds. Living in the Isles of Scilly, with its abundant maritime life, it is surprising that she did not include more of them in her collection. As she says, the species is plentiful in the Islands, and she evidently knows about their habits and behaviour from personal observation. The Isles of Scilly, incidentally, represent almost the southernmost limit of this primarily Arctic species.

Puffin *Fratercula arctica*

If Fanny were to return today to her old haunts in the Isles of Scilly she would find the Puffin population sadly reduced, as it has on all southern coasts of England. The reason is unknown.

The holes in which the birds nest are often dug into soft earth by the Puffins themselves, though they will also use old rabbit or shearwater burrows. Usually only one egg is laid, not two as Fanny states, although there are occasionally two. The species is, of course, now fully protected, but it is interesting to note that in Fanny's time the eggs were collected for food and were regarded as a delicacy.

31

British Birds

from

Nature

by

Frances Mary Isabella Smith

But who can paint
Like Nature? Can imagination boast
Amid its gay creation, hues like hers?
Or can it mix them with that matchless skill
And lose them in each other as appears
In every bud that blowes?

Thomsons Spring
page 470

afterwards Mrs Le MARCHANT

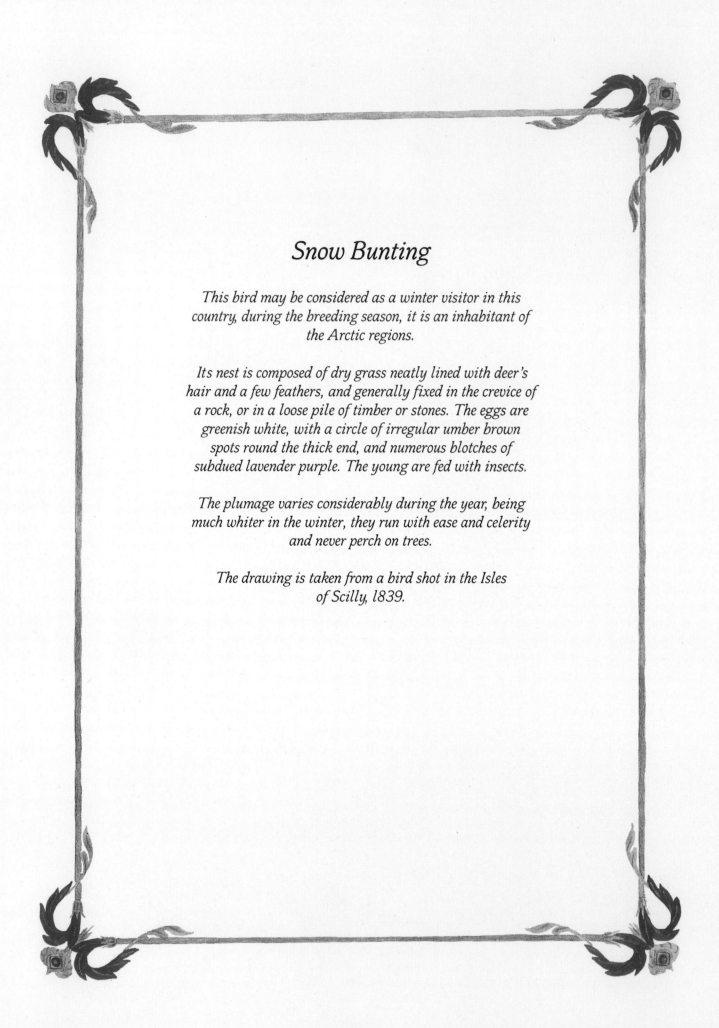

Snow Bunting

This bird may be considered as a winter visitor in this country, during the breeding season, it is an inhabitant of the Arctic regions.

Its nest is composed of dry grass neatly lined with deer's hair and a few feathers, and generally fixed in the crevice of a rock, or in a loose pile of timber or stones. The eggs are greenish white, with a circle of irregular umber brown spots round the thick end, and numerous blotches of subdued lavender purple. The young are fed with insects.

The plumage varies considerably during the year, being much whiter in the winter, they run with ease and celerity and never perch on trees.

The drawing is taken from a bird shot in the Isles of Scilly, 1839.

SNOW BUNTING.

F. Smith fecit. 1835.

Reed Bunting

The black headed or Reed Bunting is an inhabitant of marshy grounds, sides of rivers or canals, water meadows and osier beds, also at times in stubble localities. The male during the breeding season may be seen perched on a conspicuous spray, amusing himself and mate with his song, consisting of two or three notes, for an hour together.

The nest is generally placed on the ground among coarse long grass or rushes, at the foot of a thorn on the side of a canal or river; it is composed of a little moss with coarse grass, lined with finer grasses and hair. The eggs are 4 or 5 in number, of a pale brownish purple streaked with darker purple brown. Occasionally a second brood is hatched in July, the first being in May.

Their food consists of grain, insects and their larvae. In winter they form into flocks, visiting gardens, barn and stock yards. The female is smaller than the male, the head and ear coverts reddish brown varied with darker brown. On the chin on either side a descending streak of dark brown . . . and the under surface of the body more clouded. Young birds resemble the females.

This bird was drawn from one shot on the banks of the Severn.

REED BUNTING

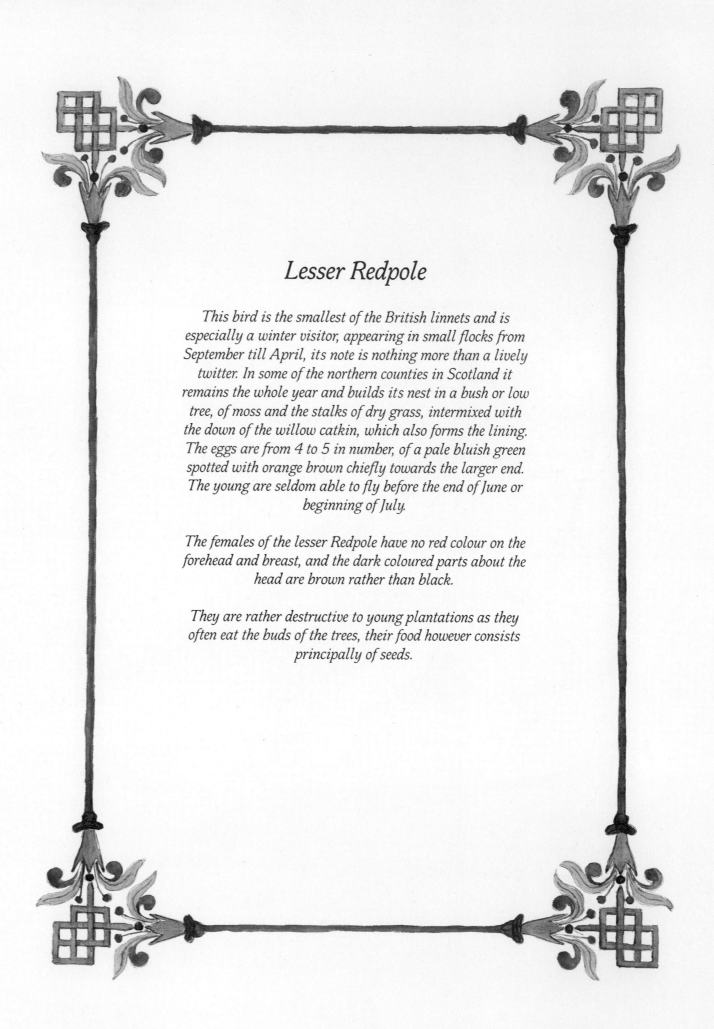

Lesser Redpole

This bird is the smallest of the British linnets and is especially a winter visitor, appearing in small flocks from September till April, its note is nothing more than a lively twitter. In some of the northern counties in Scotland it remains the whole year and builds its nest in a bush or low tree, of moss and the stalks of dry grass, intermixed with the down of the willow catkin, which also forms the lining. The eggs are from 4 to 5 in number, of a pale bluish green spotted with orange brown chiefly towards the larger end. The young are seldom able to fly before the end of June or beginning of July.

The females of the lesser Redpole have no red colour on the forehead and breast, and the dark coloured parts about the head are brown rather than black.

They are rather destructive to young plantations as they often eat the buds of the trees, their food however consists principally of seeds.

LESSER REDPOLE

Common Linnet

The male bird undergoes considerable changes in its plumage during the year; it is here represented in its summer dress, after the breeding season it loses the red on the head and breast, and during the winter the former becomes dark brown, as likewise the back, wings and tail coverts, and the latter pale wood brown with longitudinal streaks of dark brown.

They are generally seen in flocks on commons and uncultivated grounds feeding upon small seeds, and perching on the topmost twigs of furze in the thickest parts of which they generally form their nests consisting of small twigs with bents of grass, lined with wool, hair or feathers. The eggs are 4 or 5 in number of a pale bluish white speckled with pale purple and reddish spots, the young birds resemble the female .

This drawing was taken from nature in the Isles of Scilly, where they abound, July 1843.

40

RED BREASTED LINNET. male & female.

F. Smith. pinx. 1843.

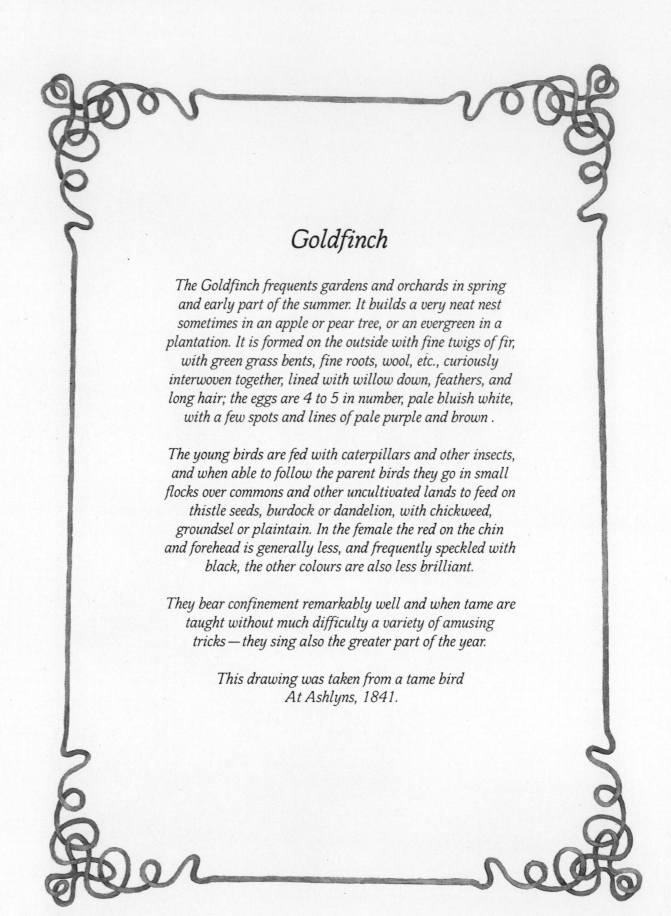

Goldfinch

The Goldfinch frequents gardens and orchards in spring and early part of the summer. It builds a very neat nest sometimes in an apple or pear tree, or an evergreen in a plantation. It is formed on the outside with fine twigs of fir, with green grass bents, fine roots, wool, etc., curiously interwoven together, lined with willow down, feathers, and long hair; the eggs are 4 to 5 in number, pale bluish white, with a few spots and lines of pale purple and brown .

The young birds are fed with caterpillars and other insects, and when able to follow the parent birds they go in small flocks over commons and other uncultivated lands to feed on thistle seeds, burdock or dandelion, with chickweed, groundsel or plaintain. In the female the red on the chin and forehead is generally less, and frequently speckled with black, the other colours are also less brilliant.

They bear confinement remarkably well and when tame are taught without much difficulty a variety of amusing tricks — they sing also the greater part of the year.

This drawing was taken from a tame bird
At Ashlyns, 1841.

GOLDFINCH.

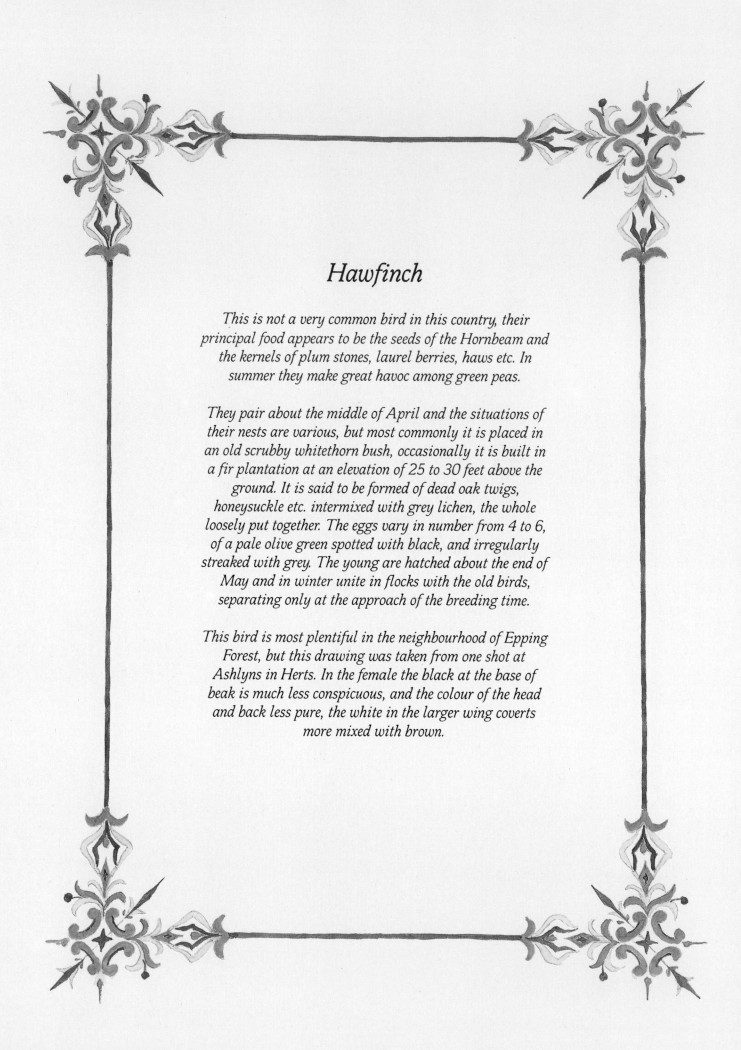

Hawfinch

This is not a very common bird in this country, their principal food appears to be the seeds of the Hornbeam and the kernels of plum stones, laurel berries, haws etc. In summer they make great havoc among green peas.

They pair about the middle of April and the situations of their nests are various, but most commonly it is placed in an old scrubby whitethorn bush, occasionally it is built in a fir plantation at an elevation of 25 to 30 feet above the ground. It is said to be formed of dead oak twigs, honeysuckle etc. intermixed with grey lichen, the whole loosely put together. The eggs vary in number from 4 to 6, of a pale olive green spotted with black, and irregularly streaked with grey. The young are hatched about the end of May and in winter unite in flocks with the old birds, separating only at the approach of the breeding time.

This bird is most plentiful in the neighbourhood of Epping Forest, but this drawing was taken from one shot at Ashlyns in Herts. In the female the black at the base of beak is much less conspicuous, and the colour of the head and back less pure, the white in the larger wing coverts more mixed with brown.

F. Smith *pinx*.

HAWFINCH

Bullfinch

The Bullfinch is a common bird, frequenting gardens, orchards, and cultivated grounds. It is rather shy and retiring in its habits, and seldom associates with any but its own species. It is found to be very destructive in gardens during the Spring, devouring the blossom buds on the fruit trees. In winter they feed on hips, haws, berries and seeds.

The nest is built about the beginning of May, and is formed of small twigs lined with fibrous roots, not very compactly twined together, generally in thick bushes. They have but one brood in the season and are believed like some other species to pair for life. The eggs are 4 or 5 in number, of a pale blue, speckled and streaked with purplish grey and dark purple, they are hatched towards the end of May after fifteen days incubation.

Bullfinches are more easily tamed than most other birds, especially taken from the nest when just fledged, they can be taught a variety of notes, as well as to whistle a little tune without much trouble. The Germans teach them to pipe by means of a little bird organ or flageolet.

The young birds in their first plumage resemble the female which is the upper bird in the drawing. They were drawn from a pair of birds at Ashlyns.

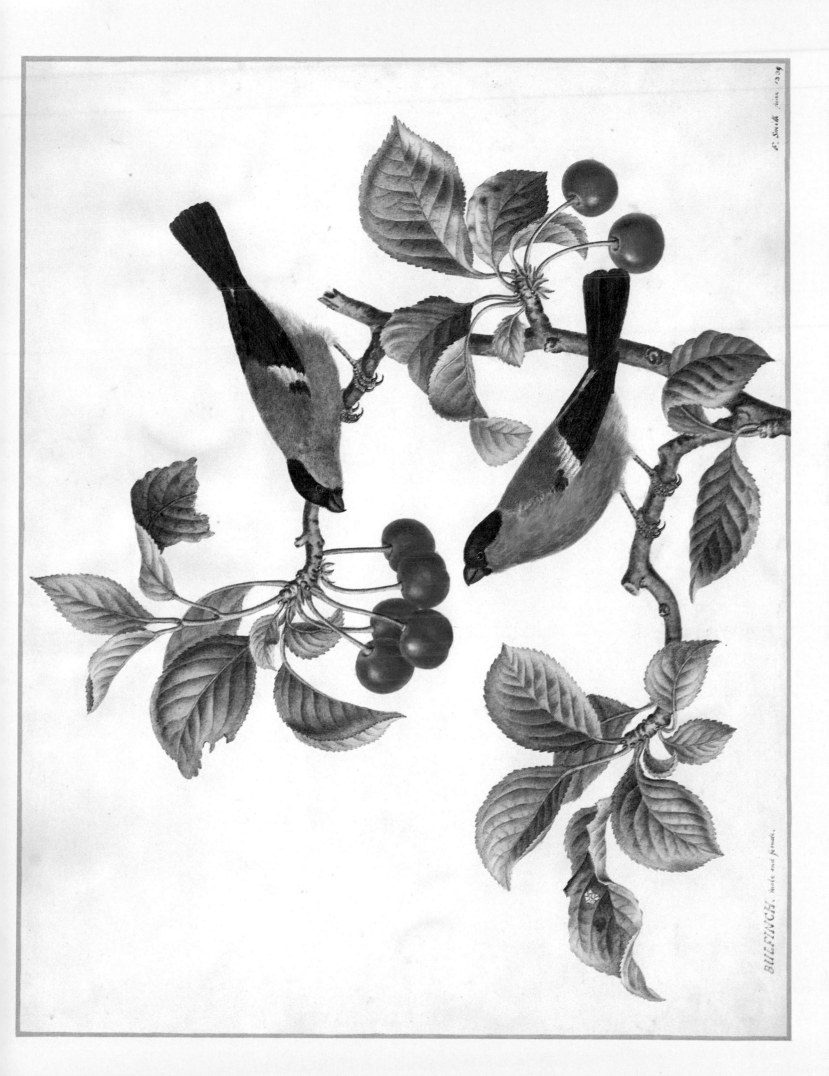

Bramble Finch

Or Mountain Finch is a winter visitor to this country and are generally seen in flocks, feeding on beech masts, grain, and other matter found on stubble lands. They are not known to have bred in this country.

In the spring the brown tip of the feathers on the head and neck are lost, those parts becoming of a fine velvet black, and the beak during the spring and summer turning a lead blue.

The female in winter has less black on the top of the head, cheek coverts and neck, dull brownish grey, with the dark line dividing the side from the nape of the neck, and the other colours of the body less pure.

The bird from which the drawing is taken was shot at Ashlyns, Hertfordshire.

Chaffinch

The Chaffinch is one of our commonest birds. In Autumn they are gregarious, frequenting hedgerows and the stubbles of corn fields, in winter if the weather is severe, they assemble about houses, gardens, etc., roosting amongst evergreens and thick hedgerows. Their flight like most of the finches is undulatory, and their food, insects, with some young and tender vegetables, in spring and summer, at other seasons, grain and seeds.

The finches are remarkable for the neatness and beauty of their nests, that of the Chaffinch, the outside is composed of moss, studded with white or green lichen, the inside is lined with wool and this again covered with hair and some feathers. The place chosen is variable, sometimes fixed in the fork of a hedgerow bush, on a branch of a wall fruit tree, frequently in apple or pear tree several feet above the ground.

The eggs usually 4 to 5 in number of a pale purplish buff, sparingly streaked and spotted with dark reddish brown.

The female has the upper surface of the body mixed with dull brown, the under part is also of a dull fawn colour and the white bars on the wings less conspicuous.

BRAMBLE FINCH

F. Smith fec.

CHAFFINCH male bird

F. Le Marchant pinx. 1869.

Tree Sparrow

The Tree Sparrow is a rare species in the southern counties of England, it has a monotonous chirp like the common Sparrow, and is an active lively bird. They build in various places, in the holes of decayed pollards, as well as in the thatch of a barn or in the deserted nests of Magpies, and Crows; their nests are formed of hay, lined with feathers.

The eggs are from 4 to 6 in number of a dull white speckled all over with light ash brown, the young are fed with soft vegetables and insects, which form the food of the parent birds in summer, at other times they feed on seeds and grain.

The female is smaller than the male and the plumage though the same is less brilliant.

This bird was drawn from one shot in Worcestershire.

Common Sparrow

This well known and most impudent bird pairs early in the season, at which time great animosity and numerous contests occur for the choice and possession of their nests, they are formed under caves of tiles, ivy covered walls, orifices of old water pipes, or any cavity sufficiently large to contain the mass of hay and feathers of which it is built. The eggs are white spotted and streaked with ash coloured and dusky brown and the first batch usually consists of 5 or 6 eggs. Two others are often produced in the season.

They build also occasionally in apple and plum trees in gardens, when thus found it is formed with a dome, and entered by a hole in the side.

White and Buff coloured varieties of this bird are not uncommon.

TREE SPARROW

HOUSE SPARROW
male & female

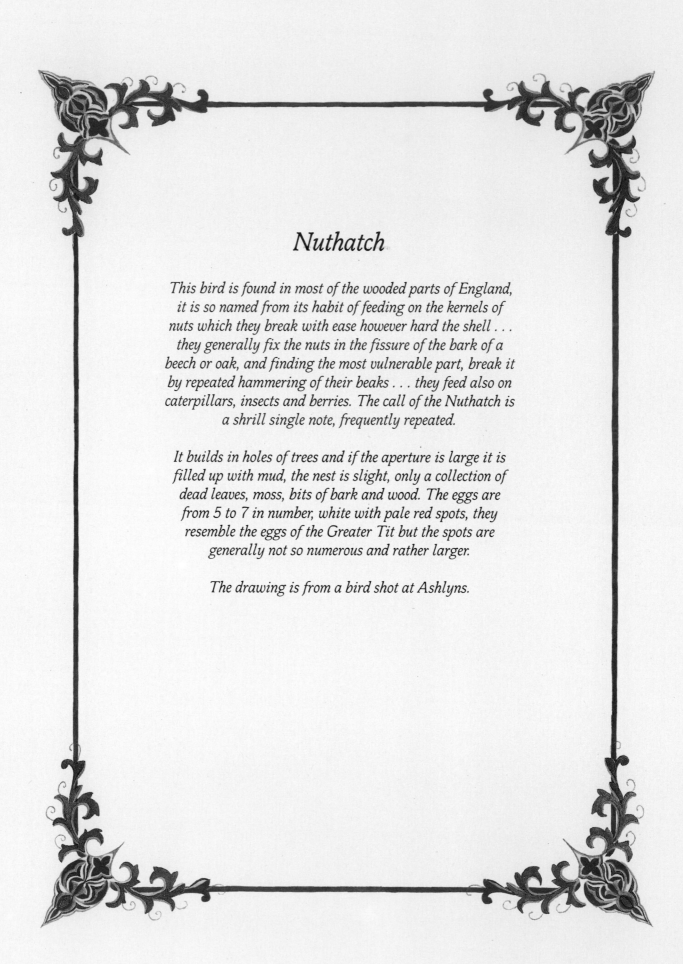

Nuthatch

This bird is found in most of the wooded parts of England, it is so named from its habit of feeding on the kernels of nuts which they break with ease however hard the shell . . . they generally fix the nuts in the fissure of the bark of a beech or oak, and finding the most vulnerable part, break it by repeated hammering of their beaks . . . they feed also on caterpillars, insects and berries. The call of the Nuthatch is a shrill single note, frequently repeated.

It builds in holes of trees and if the aperture is large it is filled up with mud, the nest is slight, only a collection of dead leaves, moss, bits of bark and wood. The eggs are from 5 to 7 in number, white with pale red spots, they resemble the eggs of the Greater Tit but the spots are generally not so numerous and rather larger.

The drawing is from a bird shot at Ashlyns.

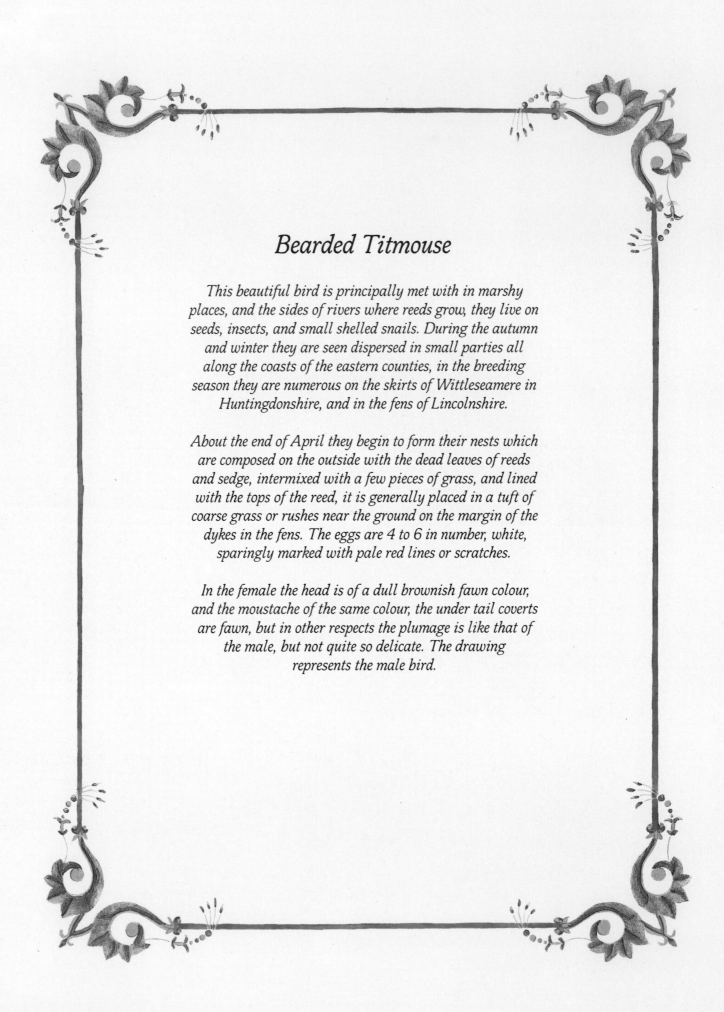

Bearded Titmouse

This beautiful bird is principally met with in marshy places, and the sides of rivers where reeds grow, they live on seeds, insects, and small shelled snails. During the autumn and winter they are seen dispersed in small parties all along the coasts of the eastern counties, in the breeding season they are numerous on the skirts of Wittleseamere in Huntingdonshire, and in the fens of Lincolnshire.

About the end of April they begin to form their nests which are composed on the outside with the dead leaves of reeds and sedge, intermixed with a few pieces of grass, and lined with the tops of the reed, it is generally placed in a tuft of coarse grass or rushes near the ground on the margin of the dykes in the fens. The eggs are 4 to 6 in number, white, sparingly marked with pale red lines or scratches.

In the female the head is of a dull brownish fawn colour, and the moustache of the same colour, the under tail coverts are fawn, but in other respects the plumage is like that of the male, but not quite so delicate. The drawing represents the male bird.

Long Tailed Titmouse

This little bird is well known, and very generally seen whereever there are thickets, shrubberies and tall hedges. It is active and lively and almost incesssantly in motion. Its food appears to be entirely of insects and their larvae. The nest is nearly oval in shape with one small hole in the upper part of the side, by which the bird enters. The outside of it sparkles with silver coloured lichens adhering to a firm texture of moss and wool, the inside is lined profusely with soft feathers. The nest is generally placed in a thick bush, and so firmly fixed that it is often found necessary to cut the branch to obtain it. The female is known to be the nest maker, in which she deposits from l0 to l2 eggs, sometimes more, they are small and white, with a few pale red specks, frequently they are quite plain.

The young family keep with their parents during their first autumn and winter, and generally crowd close together at roosting time. This bird has several notes, on the sound of which they assemble. The female is like the male in plumage with a little more black generally on the head.

This drawing was taken from one shot at Ashlyns, l838.

LONG TAILED TITMOUSE.

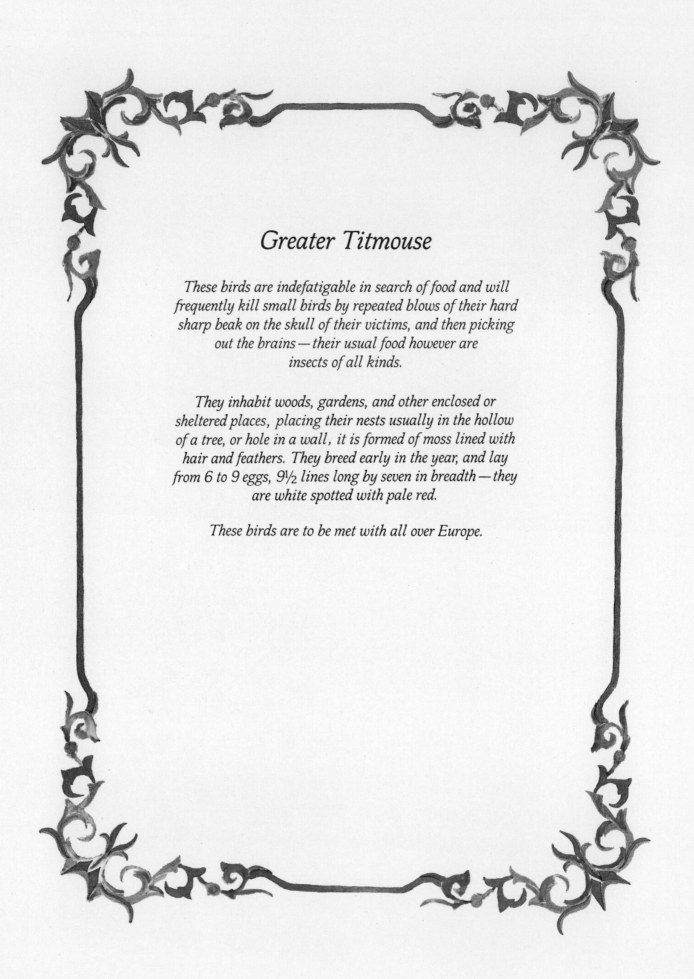

Greater Titmouse

These birds are indefatigable in search of food and will
frequently kill small birds by repeated blows of their hard
sharp beak on the skull of their victims, and then picking
out the brains — their usual food however are
insects of all kinds.

They inhabit woods, gardens, and other enclosed or
sheltered places, placing their nests usually in the hollow
of a tree, or hole in a wall, it is formed of moss lined with
hair and feathers. They breed early in the year, and lay
from 6 to 9 eggs, $9\frac{1}{2}$ lines long by seven in breadth — they
are white spotted with pale red.

These birds are to be met with all over Europe.

GREATER TITMOUSE.

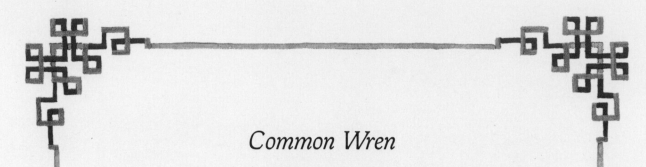

Common Wren

This little favourite sings through the greater part of the year with a shrill lively strain. It produces two broods in the season and begins to build very early in the Spring, sometimes under the thatch of a building, side of a moss covered tree, or close to an impending bank, so that the nest is sheltered from rain. The materials are generally adapted to the place, such as if against a hay stack it is made of hay, or if in a mossy tree of moss.

The nest is large for the size of the bird, generally oval in shape, domed over the top, with a small hole on one side, it is lined with feathers. The eggs are from 7 to 11 in number, sometimes more; they are either white with a few pale red spots, or all white. Its food is insects and worms. The female is smaller than the male and of a redder tinge.

Lesser Titmouse

This bird frequents in summer, small woods, orchards, gardens etc., and are said to do mischief to the young buds, which they search closely for insects which they destroy in great numbers, as well as their larvae. In winter they take to farmyards and outhouses, picking up small seeds and portions of vegetable matter.

The call note is a single shrill chirp. It builds in a hole of a wall or tree, forming its nest of a profusion of moss, hair and feathers; the eggs are very numerous, generally from 8 to 10 but as many as 18 has been recorded. They are white spotted with pale red, 7½ lines long by 6 lines broad. The female defends her nest with great courage, puffing out her feathers and hissing like an angry kitten.

COMMON WREN.
&
LESSER TITMOUSE.

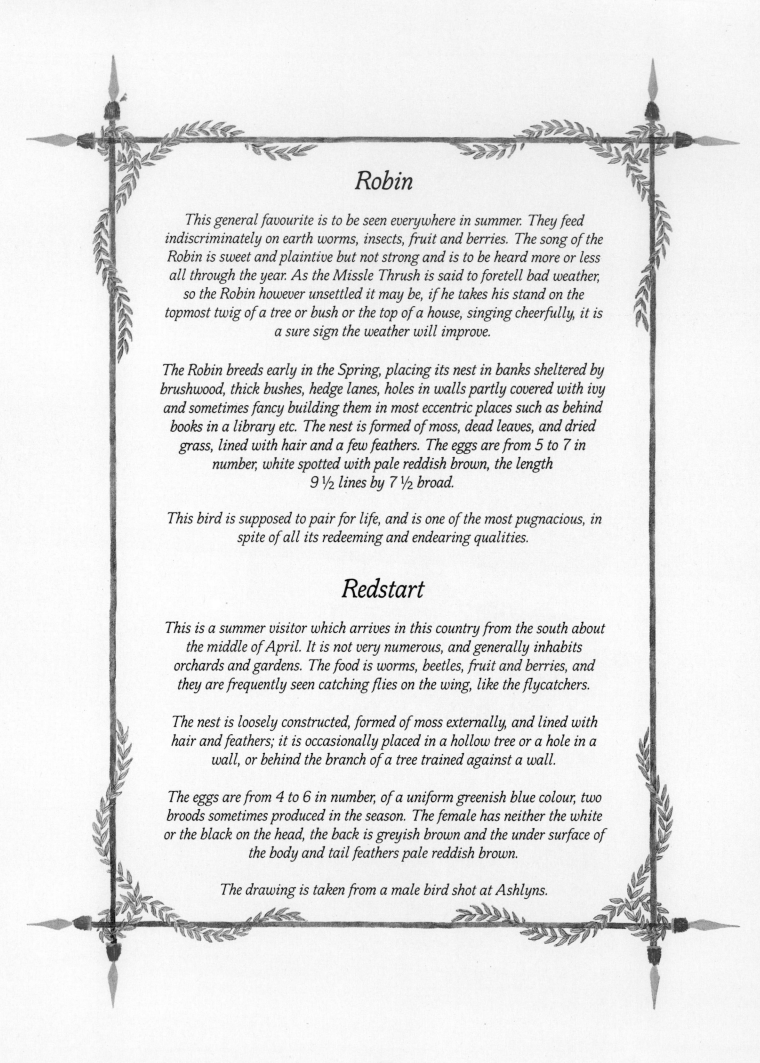

Robin

This general favourite is to be seen everywhere in summer. They feed indiscriminately on earth worms, insects, fruit and berries. The song of the Robin is sweet and plaintive but not strong and is to be heard more or less all through the year. As the Missle Thrush is said to foretell bad weather, so the Robin however unsettled it may be, if he takes his stand on the topmost twig of a tree or bush or the top of a house, singing cheerfully, it is a sure sign the weather will improve.

The Robin breeds early in the Spring, placing its nest in banks sheltered by brushwood, thick bushes, hedge lanes, holes in walls partly covered with ivy and sometimes fancy building them in most eccentric places such as behind books in a library etc. The nest is formed of moss, dead leaves, and dried grass, lined with hair and a few feathers. The eggs are from 5 to 7 in number, white spotted with pale reddish brown, the length 9 ½ lines by 7 ½ broad.

This bird is supposed to pair for life, and is one of the most pugnacious, in spite of all its redeeming and endearing qualities.

Redstart

This is a summer visitor which arrives in this country from the south about the middle of April. It is not very numerous, and generally inhabits orchards and gardens. The food is worms, beetles, fruit and berries, and they are frequently seen catching flies on the wing, like the flycatchers.

The nest is loosely constructed, formed of moss externally, and lined with hair and feathers; it is occasionally placed in a hollow tree or a hole in a wall, or behind the branch of a tree trained against a wall.

The eggs are from 4 to 6 in number, of a uniform greenish blue colour, two broods sometimes produced in the season. The female has neither the white or the black on the head, the back is greyish brown and the under surface of the body and tail feathers pale reddish brown.

The drawing is taken from a male bird shot at Ashlyns.

ROBIN

REDSTART

Stone Chat

This bird is common in various parts of England and Ireland. It frequents most of our dry commons and heaths, almost always perched on the most elevated part of a stone or twig of low bush or furze, seldom remaining long in one spot, uttering constantly its little brazen though pleasing note. Their food consists principally of worms and insects.

The Stonechat begins to build early in April. The nest is rather large for the size of the bird, and is usually placed on or near the ground at the base of some low bush. The outside is formed of moss and strong grass, lined with fine bents, hairs, and a few small feathers; the female lays about the middle or end of April 5 or 6 eggs of a pale greyish blue, the larger end minutely speckled with dull reddish brown, the length of the egg is about $8\frac{1}{2}$ lines by 7 in breadth. The young are hatched about the middle of May and in their nestling plumage have the upper parts of a greyish brown with a spot of white at the end of the feathers, after the first moult they resemble adult females.

The drawing represents both male and female, and were shot in the Scilly Isles.

STONE CHAT.

male & female

F. Smith *fect* - 1843

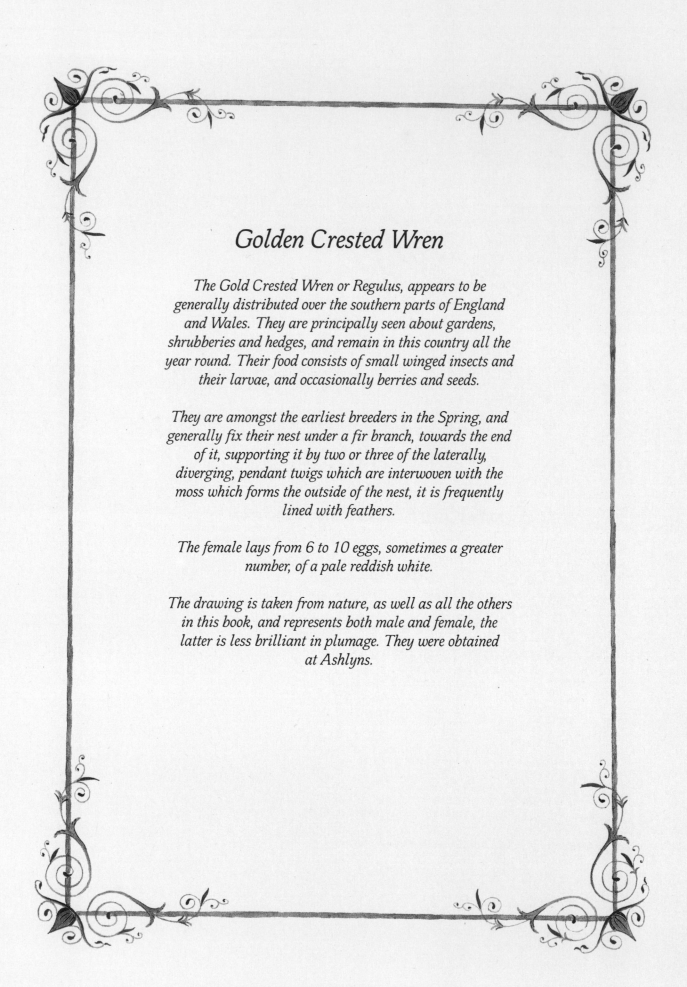

Golden Crested Wren

The Gold Crested Wren or Regulus, appears to be
generally distributed over the southern parts of England
and Wales. They are principally seen about gardens,
shrubberies and hedges, and remain in this country all the
year round. Their food consists of small winged insects and
their larvae, and occasionally berries and seeds.

They are amongst the earliest breeders in the Spring, and
generally fix their nest under a fir branch, towards the end
of it, supporting it by two or three of the laterally,
diverging, pendant twigs which are interwoven with the
moss which forms the outside of the nest, it is frequently
lined with feathers.

The female lays from 6 to 10 eggs, sometimes a greater
number, of a pale reddish white.

The drawing is taken from nature, as well as all the others
in this book, and represents both male and female, the
latter is less brilliant in plumage. They were obtained
at Ashlyns.

P. Smith delin. 1832.

DIVONIA Geranium.

GOLDEN crested WREN. male & female.

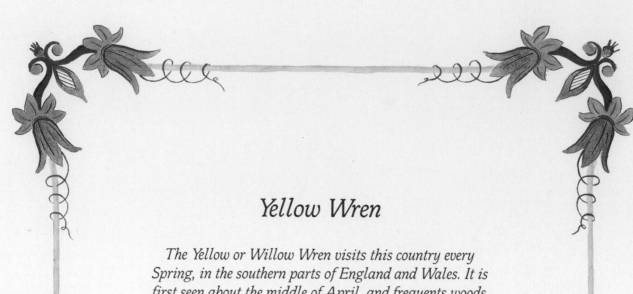

Yellow Wren

*The Yellow or Willow Wren visits this country every
Spring, in the southern parts of England and Wales. It is
first seen about the middle of April, and frequents woods,
plantations, thick hedgerows, and bushes on commons. The
food of this species is flies, aphides and insects, and not
fruit; its song, though possessing little variety, is soft and
pleasing, sometimes given from the top of a high tree and
occasionally while on the wing.*

*The nest is built on the ground, most commonly on a woody
hedge bank, among long grass and coarse herbage. It is
oval or rounded in form, composed externally of moss and
grass with a hole in the side through which the bird creeps.
It is lined with feathers. The eggs are 6 to 7 in number,
white with numerous specks of pale red — they have been
seen of a pure unspotted white — the young are hatched by
the end of May or beginning of June.*

The drawing is taken from one shot at Ashlyns, 1840.

YELLOW WREN.

White throat

This bird is plentiful during the summer in the southern
counties of England, and northern parts of Europe, arriving
about the end of April, and wintering in the more southern
countries of Europe.

The nest is sometimes placed in low brambles, bushes, and
tangled masses of long grass, generally near the ground,
but seldom more than 3 ft. above it. The outside is formed
almost entirely of dried grass stems, the sides very thin,
lined with finer bents, and a few flowery heads of grass.
The eggs are 4 to 5 in number of a greenish white ground,
spotted and speckled with ash brown and two shades of
ash green.

The food consists of insects in their various states,
especially white caterpillars, and most of the small sized
fruit and berries. The notes of the bird are rather harsh, but
sometimes pleasing.

The drawing represents a part of a balcony at Ashlyns,
where this bird was procured.

F Smith. junr. 1840.

WHITE THROAT.

Blackcap

This bird arrives in England about the middle of April, and leaves in September. They frequent woods, thick hedges, gardens etc., they are restless, timid and shy. The nest is usually placed in a bush about two or three feet from the ground and formed of bents and dried herbage, lined with fibrous roots and hair. The eggs are mostly five in number, of a pale greenish white mottled with light brown and ash colour, with a few streaks of darker brown.

The song of this bird is only inferior to that of the nightingale. They feed on berries, insects and fruit and are very partial to raspberries and currants.

This drawing represents both Male and Female, the former having the black head. They were shot at Ashlyns in Hertfordshire.

F. Smith. fecit

BLACK CAP
male & female.

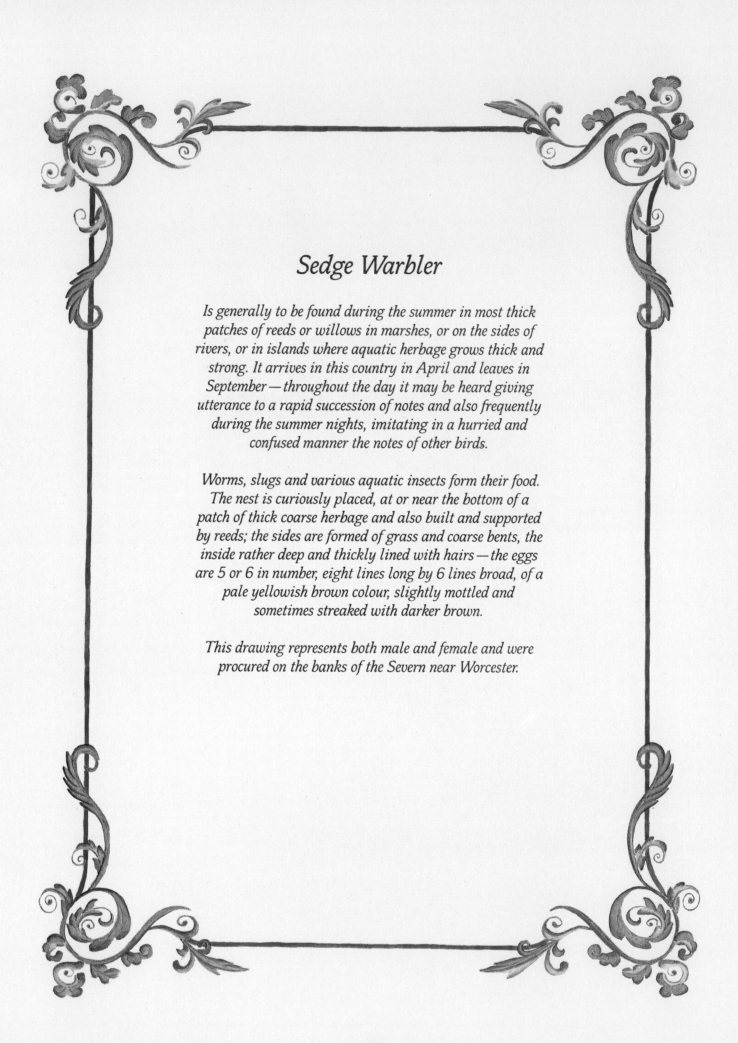

Sedge Warbler

Is generally to be found during the summer in most thick patches of reeds or willows in marshes, or on the sides of rivers, or in islands where aquatic herbage grows thick and strong. It arrives in this country in April and leaves in September—throughout the day it may be heard giving utterance to a rapid succession of notes and also frequently during the summer nights, imitating in a hurried and confused manner the notes of other birds.

Worms, slugs and various aquatic insects form their food. The nest is curiously placed, at or near the bottom of a patch of thick coarse herbage and also built and supported by reeds; the sides are formed of grass and coarse bents, the inside rather deep and thickly lined with hairs—the eggs are 5 or 6 in number, eight lines long by 6 lines broad, of a pale yellowish brown colour, slightly mottled and sometimes streaked with darker brown.

This drawing represents both male and female and were procured on the banks of the Severn near Worcester.

SEDGE WARBLER   *male & female*

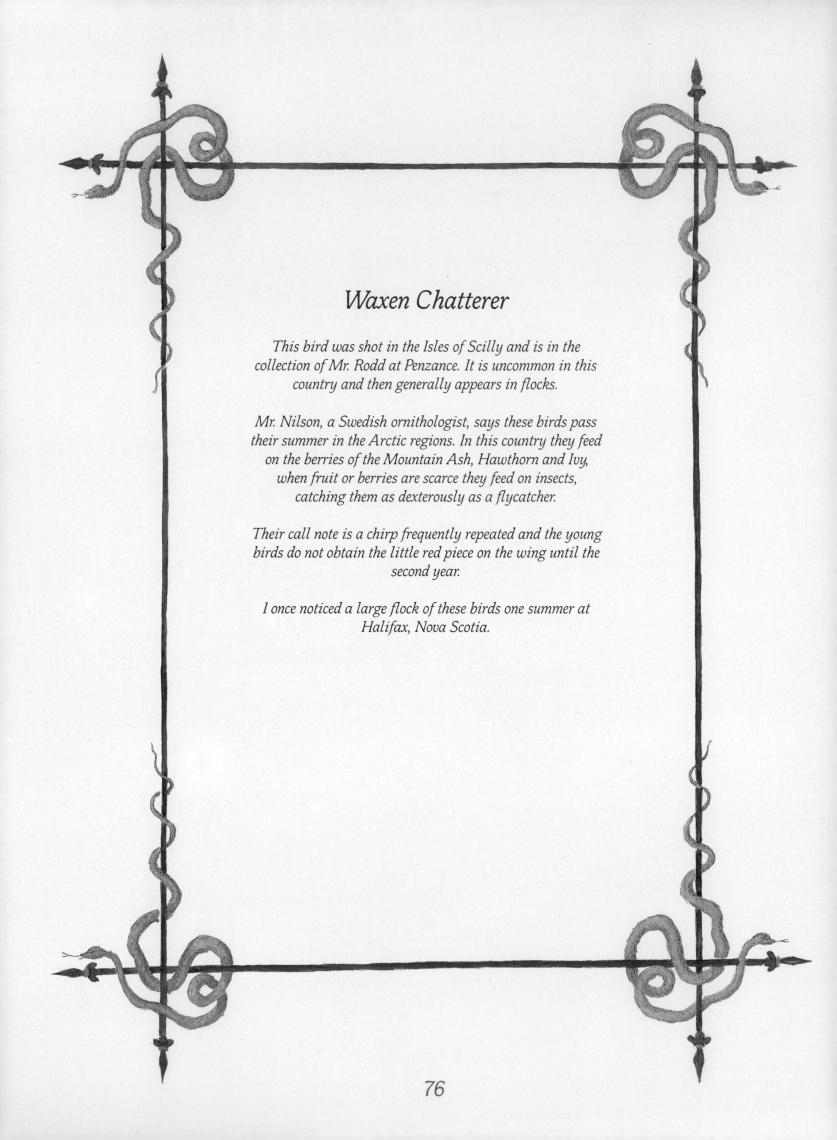

Waxen Chatterer

This bird was shot in the Isles of Scilly and is in the collection of Mr. Rodd at Penzance. It is uncommon in this country and then generally appears in flocks.

Mr. Nilson, a Swedish ornithologist, says these birds pass their summer in the Arctic regions. In this country they feed on the berries of the Mountain Ash, Hawthorn and Ivy, when fruit or berries are scarce they feed on insects, catching them as dexterously as a flycatcher.

Their call note is a chirp frequently repeated and the young birds do not obtain the little red piece on the wing until the second year.

I once noticed a large flock of these birds one summer at Halifax, Nova Scotia.

WAXEN CHATTERER

Rose Pastor

This is an accidental visitor to this country and was first noticed by Edwards, who killed his first specimen at Norwood, but several others have been obtained in various parts of England, among which is the bird here represented and taken from one shot in the Isles of Scilly, and now in the collection of Mr. Rodd at Penzance.

These birds fly in flocks in the countries in which they are common, insects appear to be the principal food, but they are also partial to fruit. They build their nests like the Starlings in holes of trees and cavities of old walls, but the colour of the eggs is not recorded.

ROSE COLOURED PASTOR

Grey Wagtail

This bird is far less numerous than the Pied Wagtail. It is seldom seen
except about marshes and water meadows, they are somewhat solitary in
their habits, shifting from place to place with undulating flight or running
with rapid steps in search of the various insects on which they
principally feed.

The nest of this bird is placed on the ground, seldom distant from a stream,
and concealed by the inequalities of the ground. It is formed of fibrous roots
and moss, lined with wool, hair or feathers; the eggs are from 5 to 6 in
number, yellowish white mottled with pale brown varying sometimes to a
darker tint, they are about 8½ lines in length and 7 lines in breadth.

In the summer the male bird has the six central tail feathers black, with
yellowish edges at the base and the chin and throat also black, the other
parts of the bird as depicted in the drawing, which represents the
winter plumage.

The colours of the female are paler than those of the male without the black
in the summer.

Yellow Wagtail

Or Ray's Wagtail is a constant visitor to this country in the summer,
appearing about the end of March or beginning of April, and leaves our
southern shores in September. It frequents arable lands, fields of peas and
tares, and young corn, also open downs, sheep pastures and meadows.

The nest is placed on the ground and is generally formed of dried bents and
fibrous roots, lined with hair. The eggs are from 4 to 6 in number, of a
whitish colour mottled nearly all over with yellow brown and ash brown.

The call note of this bird is shriller than that of the other wagtails,
consisting of two notes.

The plumage of the female is less rich in colour than that of the male, the
back being tinged with a darker brown.

This bird was shot at New Lodge near
Great Berkhamstead, Herts.

GREY WAGTAIL...

F Smith pinx.

YELLOW WAGTAIL

F Smith Var

Meadow Pepit

This is the smallest and most common of this species. It inhabits commons and waste lands and may also be found in meadows and marsh places, it seeks its food on the ground, running nimbly in pursuit of insects, worms and slugs.

The nest is built on the ground generally among grass, the outside is formed of dried bents, lined with finer bents; the eggs are from 4 to 6 in number of a reddish brown colour mottled with darker brown, it is 9 lines long by 7 broad.

The drawing represents a bird shot in the Scilly Isles with a Convolvolus which covers the sand above high water mark.

MEADOW PEPIT.

F. Smith june 1843

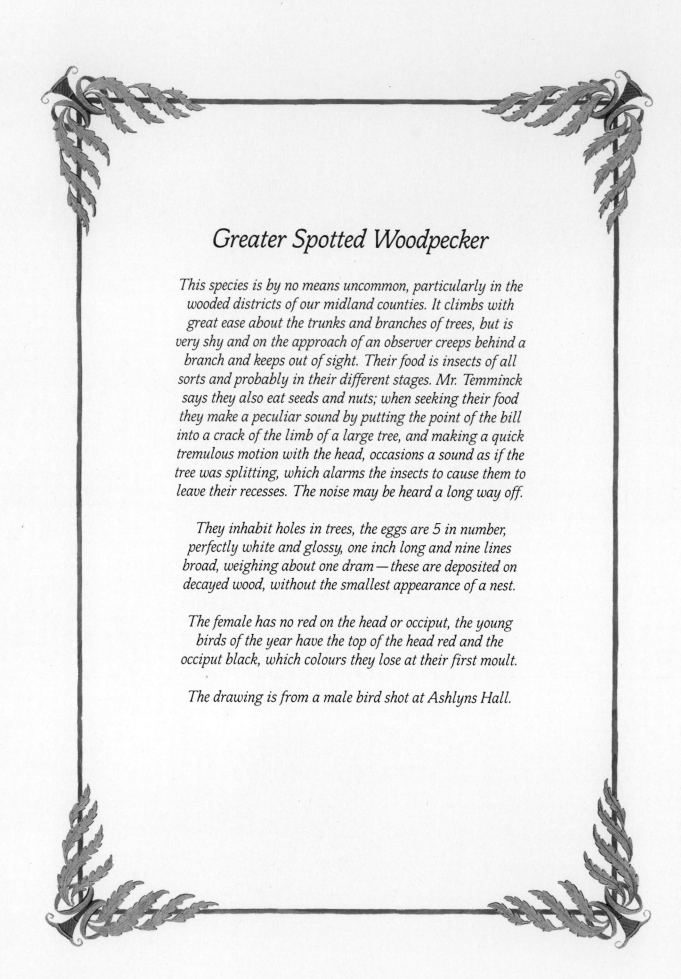

Greater Spotted Woodpecker

This species is by no means uncommon, particularly in the wooded districts of our midland counties. It climbs with great ease about the trunks and branches of trees, but is very shy and on the approach of an observer creeps behind a branch and keeps out of sight. Their food is insects of all sorts and probably in their different stages. Mr. Temminck says they also eat seeds and nuts; when seeking their food they make a peculiar sound by putting the point of the bill into a crack of the limb of a large tree, and making a quick tremulous motion with the head, occasions a sound as if the tree was splitting, which alarms the insects to cause them to leave their recesses. The noise may be heard a long way off.

They inhabit holes in trees, the eggs are 5 in number, perfectly white and glossy, one inch long and nine lines broad, weighing about one dram — these are deposited on decayed wood, without the smallest appearance of a nest.

The female has no red on the head or occiput, the young birds of the year have the top of the head red and the occiput black, which colours they lose at their first moult.

The drawing is from a male bird shot at Ashlyns Hall.

GREATER SPOTTED.

WOODPECKER.

F. Smith fecit

Roller

This bird is a native of Africa, and passes into Europe during the summer and autumn. They are to be met with in Malta, and are also said to be frequently found in the most secluded parts of the forests in Germany. Shaw in his account of Coburg describes them as being of a noisy restless disposition, the note being harsh and squalling, building their nests in the hollow of a tree, or hole in the banks of rivers. The eggs are of delicate smooth shining white almost oval in shape, one inch three lines in length by one inch one line in breadth.

The food of the Roller consists of worms, slugs, insects and berries.

The Male is distinguished by long outside tail feathers from the female, otherwise the plumage is the same. The young birds do not attain their brilliant colouring until the second year, till then the plumage is of a dull brown above and greyish green underneath.

The bird from which this drawing was made was shot in Cornwall and is in the collection of Mr. Rodd at Penzance.

Bee Eater

This is an extremely rare bird in England and is described as being a native of Africa as well as being common in the south of Europe, flying in flocks like Swallows, they are said to be gregarious both in their breeding season as in their migrations. The Bee Eater takes its food on the wing, living chiefly on winged insects, and when flying it utters a rich warbling chirp.

They excavate their holes in clayey banks, so near each other that they appear quite honeycombed, their nesting holes are lined with soft moss, and they lay from 5 to 6 eggs which are smooth white and shiny, about l inch long by 10½ lines broad. The young bird of the year has the top of the head green with a small patch of reddish brown over the eye, no red on the back, the yellow on the throat does not terminate with the dark band and the tail feathers are even at the end. The plumage of the females is not so bright as the males.

This drawing was taken from a bird shot in the Isles of Scilly and is in the collection of Mr. Rodd's British birds at Penzance, 1845.

ROLLER

BEE EATER

Kingfisher

Among our British birds none is more beautiful as to plumage, it is generally distributed throughout the country, though not very numerous anywhere. They frequent the banks of rivers or brooks, sometimes inhabiting the vicinity of fish ponds, and feed on water beetles, leeches, sticklebacks, or any other species of small fish they can seize upon by surprise.

The Kingfisher is solitary in its habits, and pugnacious in disposition, and seldom seen with any associate except its mate in the breeding season. At this time they generally take possession of a hole already formed in a bank by the water side.

The nest is formed of small fish bones, in which from 5 to 7 eggs are deposited of a short oval form, almost round, 10½ lines long, and 9 lines broad—when blown they are of a transparent white but otherwise of a delicate pink from the colour of the yolk. The young do not leave the nest till fully fledged, and have the beak wholly black. The female is similar to the male only darker and the beak rather smaller.

The bird was shot at New Lodge, Herts. 1839.

KING FISHER.

Nightjar

According to Yarret this is the only nocturnal visitor we have in this country among the summer birds. It feeds on the wing like the swallow and almost entirely on moths, cockchaffers, gnats, and caterpillars. It appears about the middle of May and leaves by the end of August or beginning of September.

They prefer moors, heaths etc. which are partially covered with bushes and patches of fern and small fir woods. They make little or no nest, but under the shelter of a bush, or taking advantage of any slight hollow in the ground, deposit two eggs, nearly oval in form, beautifully clouded and veined with blueish grey on a white ground. The young at first are covered with down, and the plumage of the female is darker than that of the male.

This drawing was made from a bird shot in the Isles of Scilly and placed on a branch of a green Aloe, the first that ever flowered there, 1845; now they are common in the islands.

F. Smith pinx 1865

NIGHTJAR
&
GREEN ALOE

Ringed Plover

This bird particularly frequents bays and sandy flats
along the coast, where the sea ebbs to a distance. They pair
in May, making no nest but depositing their 4 eggs in any
accidental depression or hollow in a bank of sand, broken
shells or shingles above high water mark.

The eggs are one inch five lines long by one inch and half a
line broad, of a pale buff or cream colour, spotted and
streaked with ash blue and black.

They feed on worms, insects, shrimps, sand hoppers and
other thin skinned crustacae. The note of this bird is a
shrill whistle.

The drawing is taken from one shot in the Isles of Scilly
where they abound, the shells are also found there.

RINGED PLOVER. ♂

F. Smith, pinx. 1865

Puffin

This drawing was taken from a bird shot in the Isles of Scilly, where they are plentiful on some of the outlaying and inaccessible rocks, one of which called the Man-a-Vaur Rock is represented in the corner.

The eggs are considered a delicacy when fresh and are deposited two only in number in holes.